Fluid Strength Yoga Practice, Vitalizing the Body and Resting the Mind
Copyright © 2017 by Faye Berton. All rights reserved.

Paperback ISBN 978-0-9990340-0-2

www.fluid-strength-yoga-practice.com

Fluid Strength Yoga Practice

Vitalizing the Body & Resting the Mind

Faye Berton

Jean Fraser | Karin Preus

LAUREL PRESS

This
practice and book
are
dedicated
to
Leela

Acknowledgments

FOR THE BOOK

This book is the result of collaboration in the finest sense.
Jean, Karin, and Maryann each have amazing skills and gifts which they
contributed with open-hearted generosity.

Jean's delicate, caring and clear-eyed touch is on every aspect of this book.
It is her words that guide the reader through the Movements. Her insistence
that the book speak directly to people's needs shaped much of the writing.

Karin's contribution speaks strongly and clearly through the
exquisite images and design that brings this practice to life.
Without them this practice could not be communicated.

Maryann was like molten gold that could be poured into the
shape of a Movement and look completely at home. Though most of us
will never have her physical clarity and elegance, we can have the
feeling of being at home in our bodies.

Through the edits of Katie Charlet and Joanne Cavallaro
my writing became the best it could be.

The magnificent image on the front cover comes through
the inspired skill of Larry Marcus.

Jean Mitchell enhanced this book through sharing her
embodied personal experience of Fluid Strength.

FOR THE FLUID STRENGTH YOGA PRACTICE™

I wove the Fluid Strength Yoga Practice out of the wisdom, knowledge and understanding that came to me through my teachers.

Swami Nijananda
Fathered me spiritually

Marjorie Barstow
Mothered me in somatic awareness

Swami Veda Bharati
Taught me how to think yogically

Moshe Feldenkrais (through his students)
Taught me how to think through my body

Dr. Vasant Lad
Taught me to think Ayurvedically

Ruthy Alon
Gave me rhythmic movement

The Fluid Strength Yoga Practice and this book exist because students experimented with the practice and shared their experiences. This created a feedback loop of teaching, learning and growing in which we all developed.

A heartfelt Thank You!

ANSEL ADAMS

Life is a challenge, meet it!
Life is a dream, realize it!
Life is a game, play it!
Life is Love, enjoy it!
SAI BABA

Table of Contents

Jean Mitchell and Joanne Cavallaro at one of Faye's Mexico retreats.
(Jean Foreward, Joanne editing)

Forward

I am a long-time student of Faye Berton at the Laurel Yoga Studio, in St. Paul, Minnesota. I had the good fortune to be present at her first Fluid Strength class and have continued weekly classes as she has developed and refined the practice.

This body of work is accessible to varying levels of fitness and experience. It has proven to be well-suited to injured or aging students who wish to develop and maintain fitness with a low risk of injury. It also attracts many students with formal dance and somatic therapy backgrounds who are attracted to Faye's unique focus on body awareness and accessing our natural ability for easy, integrated movement.

For me, this practice has been fruitful on multiple levels. The physical benefits have included maintaining strength and flexibility as well as gently resolving muscular tension and pain. I can practice the Movements with varying degrees of intensity to stimulate my energy when I'm feeling sluggish, or to calm and smooth my nerves when I'm feeling ragged.

But what keeps me intellectually intrigued and motivated is Faye's use of the Movements to work with the brain-body connection. Fluid Strength is a conversation between consciousness and body sensation. Over time this body consciousness becomes a constant companion through the routine activities of life – contributing to mindfulness, appreciation of being embodied and an overall sense of peace.

Probably the greatest revelation and joy I have received from this method is the result of the Movement-Stopping cycle. During the Stopping, prana perceptibly courses through and around my body in specific and often delightfully surprising ways. This palpably connects me to my own body's "wisdom" and I have found myself thinking: "So that's where tension and constriction needed opening!" and "Oh, even more than flesh and bones ~ I am energy, fluidity and space."

How I perceive myself and my body is often changed during the Movements. Then in Stopping, I open to receive my new self, and the possibility of all sorts of new selves. This work-rest cycle offers direct experience of the flow of change, an awareness of impermanence and the sense of infinite possibility. Stopping is a natural meditation.

Faye is a gifted, creative teacher who seems unlimited in the variations of skill and wisdom she can put into this work. Even after years of weekly classes I am always rewarded by some new awareness, knowledge, or revelation. On physical, intellectual, energetic, and spiritual levels, Faye and this method continue to deliver endless gifts. I've learned it's best to approach Fluid Strength with wide open curiosity because I never know what's going to show up. And what a nice life lesson that is.

Jean Mitchell
Retired psychologist

Is Fluid Strength for You?

A PARADIGM SHIFT

The Fluid Strength Yoga Practice is effective. It is also unique and unusual. It is a paradigm shift and by their nature paradigm shifts are interesting, enlivening, frightening and confusing. These are all common responses to Fluid Strength. Some people take to it like fish to water. Other people keep coming back, in spite of being confused, because they sense a new aliveness in themselves and their bodies.

Fluid Strength is a bottom-up process that recognizes the profound intelligence contained within the body. Fluid Strength seeks to engage this intelligence in service of achieving its goals of a vital body and a peaceful mind. In this practice we relate to the body as a wise friend and companion who offers us much in our quest for creating physical health, a nourishing relationship to life and accessing natural joy.

If you are in conversation with someone who has knowledge that you are interested in but are not familiar with, you must listen with an open mind. You put yourself out of the way for a moment so there is room in you for understanding something new, for seeing something from a different perspective. This kind of listening is needed if you are interested in connecting to the intelligence in your body. It is also how you will most benefit from what Fluid Strength has to offer.

Rilke's line "try to love the questions themselves" expresses the underlying dynamic of Fluid Strength. The Movements are done with a questioning, receptive attitude. These whole-body-awareness questions ask things like: Is my movement honest? Am I using more effort than the movement requires? Am I working "with" my body or am I trying to manipulate it? How do I allow prana to support me? Am I kind to myself when a movement is challenging? Do I trust my body?

These are embodied awareness questions, not cognitive questions. They are living questions for keeping ourselves in a happy and engaged relationship to our body, to ourselves, and to life. Through them we stay in the moment and in process. After all, life is a process!

The goal in Fluid Strength is not learning to *do* the Movements, but rather using the Movements to help ourselves *remember* integrated strength, physical freedom and a comfortable body. Movements are a means by which we cultivate qualities and dynamics that help our body to remember health and vitality. Fluid Strength is a practice of unlearning. We are looking to shed the habits that are covering our natural lightness, ease and joy.

And like any practice, Fluid Strength is not right for everyone. It is a good practice for people who are interested in embodied awareness and for people who enjoy the sacred challenge of learning and growing. Fluid Strength is beneficial for meditation practitioners because it balances the body and cultivates a different yet complimentary type of awareness.

For people who have sensitive bodies and have difficulty finding a way to safely maintain physical strength, Fluid Strength can be very helpful. This is true whether their sensitivities come from age, injuries, or genetics.

At the other end of the spectrum are dancers, athletes and even asana practitioners whose skill is achieved at the cost of natural movement being trained out of their bodies. Farther down the road it is not uncommon for these people to experience physical problems. Fluid Strength has proven itself to be beneficial in helping them regain natural, integrated movement.

Yoga practitioners who are looking to enhance their understanding of yoga in its familiar form may not find much of interest here. I have paid my dues in the study of yoga philosophy and yoga asana and I understand how they are designed to help us find health and happiness in our journey through life. Fluid Strength is rooted in the purposes and goals of traditional yoga; it is not an expression of traditional yogic form. It is Leela, it is divine play.

Faye Berton

Orientation to This Book

After 20 years of studying and practicing traditional asana, and 15 years teaching I found myself at a crossroads. I was no longer benefiting from my practice of asana. That was difficult. Faye Berton, my first yoga teacher, had just returned to the Twin Cities and was developing the Fluid Strength Yoga Practice, and it was just what I needed.

This practice encompasses all the elements of yoga – body, mind, and spirit, and I am again enjoying the fruits of yoga. The physical and emotional strength and stability it provides serves me well during even the most fretful and unsettling times. My life is imbued with the qualities of fluidity and resiliency, and moments of deep peace and calm are now the norm more than ever before.

It is with great pleasure and satisfaction that I observe my students reaping the benefits of this profound work. We are very happy to be sharing this practice with you.

This book is laid out in two sections. The first section explains the practice and its philosophical underpinnings; the second section describes how to practice.

In the first three chapters you are introduced to the unique nature of Fluid Strength along with the story of how Fluid Strength was developed by Faye Berton in response to a serious health challenge.

The second three chapters go into more detail about the dynamics of the Movements and how they create health, strength and well-being.

Because a vital spine is so important a whole chapter is given to describe the Spinal Flip. Spinal Flip is the primary Movement in Fluid Strength and is used in numerous ways to awaken the spine. Fluid Strength is imbued with neuromotor learning principles from the Feldenkrais Method® and the chapter on Neurological Cleansers gives you a direct taste of how they work.

The following three chapters discuss the importance of the resting phase of Fluid Strength. They describe the different ways resting is used in Fluid Strength with Transitional Awareness, Stopping, and the use of wisdom principles.

The final two chapters of this section bring into focus the two main pillars of Fluid Strength Yoga for the reader to refine and empower their Movements – the awareness of the midline, and the primary importance of the qualities evoked in Fluid Strength Movements.

The second section of the book provides images and clear instructions for each of the Movements, and describes how to structure a Fluid Strength practice. Four sample Practice sequences of varying lengths are included.

The final section is the Movement Index. This section gives you an overview of the Movements with descriptions of some of their unique benefits. All Movements discussed in the book appear here.

Welcome to the Fluid Strength Yoga Practice!

Jean Fraser

Leave the familiar
for a while.
Let your senses and
bodies stretch out.
HAFIZ

PART ONE

Fluid Strength Yoga

There is more wisdom in your body
than in your deepest philosophy.
FRIEDRICH NIETZSCHE

The Fluid Strength Yoga Practice

This section introduces you to the
Fluid Strength Yoga Practice through
The Story of how it developed.

What is Fluid Strength? describes
the transformational potency of
this way of doing yoga and the
different aspects that contribute
to this potency.

But It Doesn't Look Like Yoga!
offers a traditional view of yoga
and how that view is integrated
into Fluid Strength.

Faye at Iguazu Falls, Argentina

The Story

THE PROBLEM

The Fluid Strength Yoga Practice grew out of my personal need. Seven years of declining health left me depleted, weak, and unable to walk even a block.

My love of travel had come back to bite me. Somewhere in my journeys I had picked up an intense and difficult-to-diagnose parasite. Multiple rounds of parasite tests in four different countries had come back negative. It seemed that my problem was not parasites. My health, however, continued to deteriorate.

In the beginning of my eighth year of downward spiral, an astute naturopath looked at my skin and knew I had a parasite. She arranged a test with a specialty lab and within a month I had the name of the parasite that I was hosting. Shortly after that, I had a prescription for an anti-parasite medication.

Two hours after taking the medication, the daily nausea I had lived with for more than seven years had vanished. It was miraculous! My next test confirmed what I knew, my parasites were gone.

THE NEW CHALLENGE

Still, my body was deeply compromised and the next challenge was regaining my health. My diet was good and I had a great naturopath. From having trained in Ayurveda and somatic disciplines, I knew many ways to support healing. I had been teaching yoga for well over two decades and was familiar with a wide range of wellness-creating practices using the body and breath.

Despite these resources and my best efforts for the following two years, I could not regain my strength and energy.

THE DARK BEFORE THE DAWN

One morning I was sitting, exhausted and defeated, on the corner of my bed. I had no energy with which to engage the new life I was starting. I was depressed.

I started gently rocking my spine from a natural impulse to comfort myself. My breath began to entrain with the rhythm of the movement. To my surprise, when I stopped doing the movement, I felt better. I had a tiny but noticeable injection of energy. I repeated the same movement and each time I stopped, I experienced an infusion of energy.

THE ART AND SCIENCE OF REJUVENATING

My mind was lighting up. In my training I had learned about Rasayana, the branch of Ayurvedic medicine devoted to rejuvenation. In it, herbs, life-style guidelines, yoga, and food are organized in specific ways for creating longevity and returning diseased or aging bodies back to health. As I contemplated Rasayana, I realized that it is a process of combining a number of health-producing factors in a way that addresses the needs of a particular person.

Why could I not develop a physical Rasayana practice to help me regain my energy? I wanted my life back! I was experienced with yoga, Ayurveda, The Feldenkrais Method®, and Bones for Life®. The combination of these trainings gave me a rich knowledge of how to work with the body, breath, and mind. It also gave me a solid understanding of the human energy system and the dynamics of healing.

THE SPINE AND THE BREATH

I thought about the moment when the breath joined in as I was rocking my spine. It was so natural and easy. The breath and the spine are two essentials in yoga practice and are both basic to health. It was obvious they were the place to start.

I wanted to stimulate my energy so it seemed natural to use a stimulating movement. Still sitting on the corner of my bed I began to flex and extend my spine more vigorously. This time I consciously connected my breath to the movement. I moved for under a minute, but when I stopped I felt the influx of even more energy.

I began to feel a timid hope arising in my belly and chest.

I needed to explore this more. My body did not feel stable in the movement so I held my legs together from my feet to the tops of my thighs. When I moved my spine and breath using my legs in this way, I was not only more stable but the movement was easier and stronger. When I rested after the movement there was another increase in the energy I received.

In those few minutes on the corner of my bed I had identified 4 major components of a physical Rasayana practice. These became the foundation of the Fluid Strength Yoga Practice:

- Moving the spine in a vigorous, repetitive, rhythmic flexion and extension
- Merging the breath with the movement
- Keeping the legs together while moving the spine
- Resting after each movement

THE SOLUTION

I began scanning my memory for the principles and practices from yoga, Ayurveda, and Feldenkrais that I knew to have the greatest potential for healing, strengthening, and stimulating energy. What emerged was the necessity of:

- A vital, flexible spine
- A focused mind
- Engaged breath
- Digestive health
- Neuromotor exercise principles
- Deep resting
- Right alignment to life
- Surrender and receptivity
- Clear intention
- Awareness of energy (prana)
- Awareness of "how" we do things
- Balance on all levels

Everything on this list is embedded in Fluid Strength, some things overtly and others in the background. They are all completely interwoven and it is their synergy that creates the potency of this practice. This list was easy to come up with, but it has taken years for everything on it to come together into cohesive practice.

IT STARTS WITH SPINAL AWARENESS AND BREATH

Awakening the spine is a primary focus in this practice, so exploring your spine is a good place to start. The movements described below will help you get in touch with how the neck and lower back move. They are also a toe in the water to learning the primary Movement of Fluid Strength, the Spinal Flip.

⋙ FIRST ⋘

- Sit on the edge of chair with your feet flat on the floor.

- Bring the palm of your right hand to comfortably touch the back of your neck with your fingers slightly separated and gently touching the vertebrae.

The more sensitively and gently you do these Movements, the more awareness you will gain.

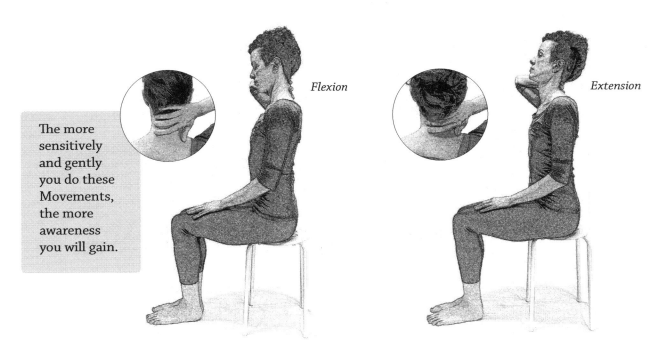

Flexion

Extension

Hand on neck

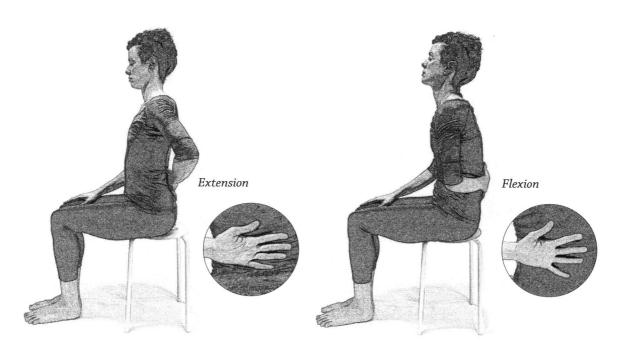

- Flex and extend your neck – bringing your chin toward the chest to flex the neck – and then lift your chin up to extend it.

- As you gently repeat this movement sense your fingers coming closer together as you lift your chin – and coming farther apart as you bring your chin toward your chest.

≫ THEN ≪

- Put the back of your left hand to touch your lower back with your fingers separated.

- As you arch your lower back forward, sense the space between your fingers decreasing. When you move your lower back backward in flexion, feel the space between your fingers increasing.

Extension

Flexion

Hand on back

Continued on next page

≫ THEN ≪

- With your right fingers on your neck and your left fingers on your lower back, simultaneously extend the neck and flex the lower back.

- Do the reverse – flex the neck and arch the lower back. Continue this movement many times using your hands to become aware of the movement of the vertebrae.

- Rest quietly with your awareness through your whole self and notice how you feel.

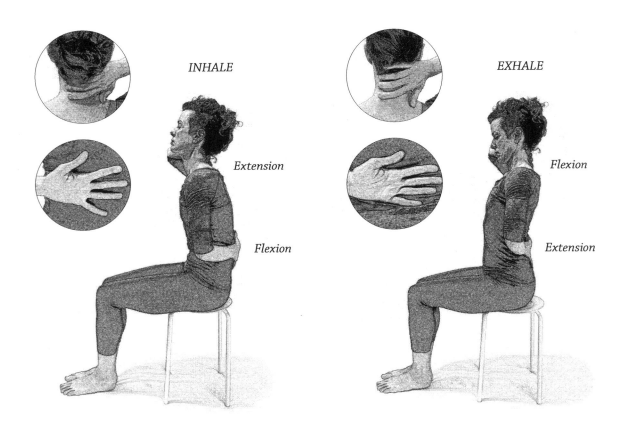

INHALE

Extension

Flexion

EXHALE

Flexion

Extension

Hands on both

※ ADD THE BREATH ※

- Once this movement feels familiar and easy, let the breath become part of it. Let the exhale come when the neck extends and the lower back flexes, and let the inhale happen when the neck flexes and the lower back extends.

- Repeat this movement softly and sensitively, looking for the feeling that the movement and breath are happening in a natural way.

- Rest quietly with your awareness through your whole self and note any new awareness of your spine.

....

These movements are for developing awareness. Doing them slowly and gently, we can say even lazily, will yield the greatest amount of awareness. For all of the years I have been working with somatic disciplines and yoga, this simple process continues to amaze me with how it awakens me to my spine in new ways.

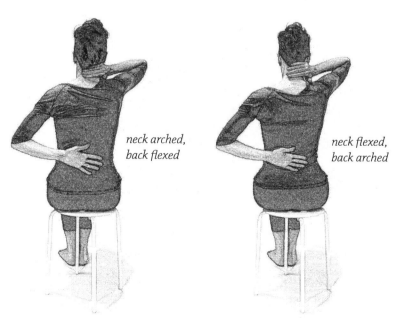

neck arched, back flexed

neck flexed, back arched

Rear view

This is your body, your greatest gift, pregnant with wisdom you do not hear, grief you thought was forgotten, and joy you have never known.
MARION WOODMAN

Awake. My dear
Be kind to your sleeping heart.
Take it out into the vast fields of Light
And let it breathe.
HAFIZ

RUTH BROPHY

What is Fluid Strength?

A HOLISTIC PRACTICE

Fluid Strength is a simple, potent holistic yoga practice. It focuses on strengthening the entire person, not just the body. It is inspired by the traditional yogic goal of awakening to our full potential. Its potency comes from combining yogic and Ayurvedic wisdom with neuromotor development principles.

Simple, rhythmic contraction and release movements infused with dynamic breathing are used to vitalize the core of the body and awaken the spine. They develop functional strength and powerfully activate our life energy (prana). Each Movement is followed by a full rest in which we become aware of the field around our body, and the awakened prana within it.

The structure of this practice is based on the traditional yoga model of doing the corpse pose after each posture. Each Fluid Strength Movement is followed by resting. Repeating the resting phase creates a profound state of inner quiet.

Fluid Strength is unique in its simplicity and potency. The functional movement patterns are made exponentially effective by merging them with intensified breathing. Alternating these Movements with stopping invites progressively deeper states of rest and rejuvenation. Engaging prana directly gives us a powerful, easily accessible tool for self-healing.

WHO IS IT FOR?

Fluid Strength is simultaneously accessible and challenging to all levels of students. Beginning students benefit from the movement patterns being simple. Highly trained people discover deeper levels of organic body intelligence and access fresh movement potential.

Most of the Movements are done lying down or sitting on the floor, making it easy for people to work within their capacity. The Movements can also easily be adapted to accommodate individual needs.

THE MOVEMENTS

Whole-body movements that mimic activities of daily life, done with greater intensity and duration, are a highly effective form of exercise. These kinds of movements challenge us to strengthen and mobilize our body in ways that we actually use it. This type of exercise develops what is referred to as *functional strength*.

The movement patterns of Fluid Strength are based on principles of functional strength. Current neuromotor research tells us that dynamic, functionally-related movements are one of the best ways of improving strength, balance, agility, and coordination.

In Fluid Strength, every Movement is done with awareness of the whole body. Combined with vigorous breath, these Movements enliven the body, awaken healing energy, and frequently result in a spontaneous release of pain.

STOPPING AND RESTING

"Stopping" is the resting phase. It is used to become aware of the energy field around the body. In yoga, this field is called the subtle body or pranic field.

Prana is our life energy, and a subtle aspect of the breath. Coupling movement with intensified breathing powerfully stimulates prana. Once stimulated, it can be felt moving through and around the body. By allowing ourselves to rest in and receive the nourishment of this enlivened energy, a deep healing and spontaneous meditation arise.

IT'S NATURAL

There is a deep ordinariness in the Fluid Strength Yoga Practice. Most of the Movements are done naturally by children in play. It is also natural for children to just stop – and drop into rest. Indeed, it is that naturalness that we are seeking to help ourselves to remember. The ordinariness of this practice, however, belies the great amount of wisdom that is embedded in it and the potency it has to help us to uncover the best of who we are.

Yesterday
I was clever
so I wanted
to change
the world.
Today
I am wise
so I want to
change myself.
RUMI

But it Doesn't Look Like Yoga!

The word yoga almost always conjures up images of people doing postures (asanas) from Indian yoga. We are very familiar with yoga from India, but less so with the yoga from Japan, Tibet, and China. Although Fluid Strength emerged organically from my experience with Indian yoga, because of its emphasis on movement, breath, energy, and healing, it more closely resembles these other forms.

Yoga in the West focuses primarily on the postures. Yoga, however, has a broad range of practices for refining the body, mind, and heart. Its goal is the awakening of our highest potential, and the postures are just one of the practices that serve this goal.

The Yoga Sutras of Patanjali is perhaps the most widely read yogic text. Its 196 concise sentences are gems of wisdom that we can spend a life-time unfolding. In them Patanjali describes the yogic journey as having eight limbs. These eight limbs are the philosophical underpinning of Fluid Strength. Their wisdom is woven through every aspect of the practice.

THE EIGHT LIMBS OF YOGA

⪼ ONE ⪻

Harmonizing Ourselves with Life offers guidelines for developing life-enhancing relationships with the people and things around us. The sense of safety, support, and connection we receive from following these guidelines gives us a solid foundation for a happy life and a fruitful yoga practice.

The most famous of these guidelines is non-violence; not creating harm or pain. People have posited that if we really explore non-violence we will find that the other guidelines are embedded in it.

An application of non-violence that is relevant in learning Fluid Strength is simply that we learn better when we feel safe. If we push ourselves physically beyond what our body can safely do, we are being violent to ourselves.

> Yoga is anything which reveals or reflects the wholeness that we truly are.
> KRISHNANANDA SARASWATI

Cultivating a non-violent relationship to ourselves is how we bring that quality of relationship to the world. Developing non-violence on different levels is an ongoing theme in Fluid Strength.

≫ TWO ≪

Relating to Self offers guidelines for cultivating a harmonious relationship with ourselves. How we relate to ourselves is the basis of how we relate to life. It colors our every experience. This limb essentially talks about cultivating a commitment to support ourselves in achieving our greatest happiness.

In seeking our happiness, we meet the edges of our comfort. This is essential. We learn to be okay with being uncomfortable and we learn to be a friend to ourselves when we are challenged.

In Fluid Strength, if we become frustrated with ourselves for not feeling competent in doing a Fluid Strength Movement, we recognize and acknowledge that fact. This acknowledgment creates the space to let us bring forward a softer and kinder relationship to ourselves.

≫ THREE ≪

Postures are used to develop a strong, flexible, and healthy body. In addition to their physical benefits, they are a natural support for a quiet mind and peaceful emotions. The Movements of Fluid Strength create similar benefits.

Different styles of yoga cultivate the body differently. Some styles are vigorous, some gentle, some emphasize challenge, while others emphasize relaxation. These differences are consistent with the yogic view that there is no single right way to practice; rather a practice should suit the individual.

Fluid Strength is interested in functional strength which includes coordination, whole-body integration, and self-awareness. The resilient aliveness in a child's body inspired the Fluid Strength view of physical health and its emphasis on springy and pliable muscles, joints, and organs.

When body, breath, and mind work together in harmony to achieve a spiritual goal, that is yoga.
BABA HARI DASS

❯❯ FOUR ❮❮

Harnessing Breath is one of the best tools for staying centered during the busyness of life. The breath is a bio-feedback system we can use to stay in touch with what is happening within us on a moment-by-moment basis. This is our medicine for reaching the end of the day with some reserves. Simply paying attention to the breath keeps us on track.

The pressure of modern living makes imbalanced breathing the norm. A common imbalance, and happily one that can be easily recognized and worked with, is a dominant inhalation. It is a breathing pattern linked to stress and anxiety. The antidote is cultivating a shorter inhalation and longer exhalation. This is not done as an exercise but rather as an intention that in time we can help the body remember this way of breathing.

Konstantin Buteyko, a Russian doctor, researched this pattern and described more than 200 health issues that he believed could be reversed by addressing this imbalance. Among these are allergies, hypertension, irritable bowel syndrome, menopausal disorders, sleep disorders, and migraines (see www.breathingcenter.com).

Breathing is center stage in Fluid Strength. There is an emphasis on a strong, clear exhalation in the Movements. During the resting phase after a Movement it is easy to sense how the breath naturally settles into the pattern of a longer exhalation and a shorter inhalation.

❯❯ FIVE ❮❮

Skillful Use of Senses is skillful use of our energy. We live in a sea of sensory stimulation and are bombarded by advertising whose intention is to use our senses in order to get our attention. Much of our life energy is lost in this way. If we become aware of this happening, we can choose to say yes or no to it. To develop this awareness, we need to know the experience of quiet senses. When the senses are quieted so also are the mind and emotions.

In Fluid Strength, a resting phase follows vigorous body/breath movements. When we finish one of these energized Movements we immediately enter into rest. In this rest the senses spontaneously become quiet. Over time we can access this quiet apart from the Movements, and bring it into our daily life.

≫ SIX ≪

Concentration is our best friend in living life and bringing our dreams to fruition. It is most commonly thought of in terms of concentrating the mind. We can, however, also concentrate the body and the breath.

Fluid Strength simultaneously concentrates all three. For example, Mermaid Legs concentrates the body by holding the legs together during a Movement. The Movement is then infused with concentrated, enlivened breathing. Holding the body and breath together in this way during a vigorous movement requires the mind to hold steady. In this way we concentrate our whole being.

I asked my teacher, Swami Nijananda a few months before he died what he considered the most important thing for yoga practice. His response was immediate and clear – *concentration*.

≫ SEVEN ≪

Meditation comes in many forms. It is essentially an aware, relaxed mind which rests in itself – free from any clinging to the thoughts that pass through. Meditation is good medicine for the excess activity and fragmentation that we face most days. It is the means by which we touch into our capacity for profound inner stillness.

Meditation in Fluid Strength arises spontaneously in Stopping. As a gift of stimulated prana, it lasts only a few minutes. Although short lived, because it is natural and effortless it gives us an honest taste of meditation. It is very nourishing on its own and is a good adjunct for a formal meditation practice.

≫ EIGHT ≪

Self-Realization is the ultimate goal of yoga. It is accessing our highest potential as human/spiritual beings. Some yoga practices have this goal in the forefront. Fluid Strength acknowledges this potential and points lightly in its direction.

....

We can benefit greatly by remembering the eight limbs. They can serve as a touchstone for what we most need in any given moment. Do we need to attend to our feelings or how we are relating to someone (limbs 1 and 2)? Maybe our body needs care or we notice that our breathing is disturbed (limbs 3 and 4). If we are fragmented, how do we access concentration (limb 5)? Maybe we need the deeper nourishment of meditation or surrendering ourselves into the mystery of life (limbs 6 and 7). Identifying what we need at a given time is the first step in taking care of ourselves.

Mastery of yoga is really measured by how it influences our day-to-day living, how it enhances our relationships, how it promotes clarity and peace of mind.
T. K. V. DESIKACHAR

Be strong then,
and enter into
your own body.
KABIR

About the Movements

This section describes the **Movements** of Fluid Strength, and how breath, rhythm and awareness are used to enliven them.

The chapter on **Spinal Flip** introduces you to the primary Movement in this practice and discusses the importance of vitalizing the spine.

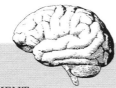

NEURO MOMENT

Befriending the Body

Our body is the instrument through which we live our lives. Just as a well-tuned musical instrument lends itself more easily to playing good music, a body that is responsive, relaxed and pain-free makes life easier and more enjoyable. Befriending the body is a key player in the Fluid Strength approach to cultivating this type of body.

In befriending the body, rather than training, exercising or controlling it, we are seeking to trust, listen to and work *with* it. We are changing our relationship with our body from that of being a slave, to being an intelligent partner.

Befriending the body is being equally interested in how we relate to ourselves while doing a Movement – as we are in the Movement itself. We notice if we are using more effort than is necessary, then reduce it. If we become self-critical in a Movement we find difficult we pause, turn that criticism into curiousness about the difficulty – and then continue. This curiosity is the first step in becoming aware of what is preventing the movement from being easy.

In this way of working we are both cultivating the Movements and becoming more self-aware. With awareness, we discover how much power we have to create a confident, comfortable body.

The Fluid Strength Movements

The Fluid Strength Movements are designed to develop strength and vitality with a minimum of effort. They enliven the body, awaken healing energy, and frequently result in a spontaneous release of pain.

Most movements are done lying down so we can be free of the effort of using anti-gravity muscles. In standing and sitting our anti-gravity habits are actively engaged. Lying down allows them to disengage, which leaves us with more energy for movement and makes it easier to learn better ways of using our body.

REFINING FLEXION AND RELEASE

All physical activity happens through the contracting and releasing of muscles. When this interplay happens easily, our body is comfortable and responsive.

Simple, repetitive contraction and release patterns are used in Fluid Strength to cultivate this essential aspect of a vital body. Some of these are large and involve the whole body, others are small and localized. In developing strong, springy contractions and the ability to easily release them, our body becomes pliable and alive.

SUPPORTED BY RHYTHM

The Movements are repeated for anywhere from 2-4 minutes, giving enough time for a clear, natural rhythm to emerge. This rhythm then effectively sustains the movement and encourages the dissolving of unneeded effort.

Rhythm is a powerful tool for healing, balancing, and harmonizing the body and mind. It is an essential support for the Fluid Strength goal of developing the body as a whole, rather than individual muscles or muscles groups.

Again and again return to where the breaths meet, fuse and transform into each other.
THE BHAIRAVA SUTRAS

BODY AND BREATH FUSION

The Movements are a fusion of an aligned body and intensified breathing. The ideal experience in doing the Movements is feeling equally that the body is moving the breath and the breath is moving the body. The breath and body are partners – each mobilizes, strengthens, and energizes the other.

The contraction and release phases of the Movements are married to the exhalation and inhalation. The exhalation happens with the contraction phase, the inhalation with the release phase. The exhale and contraction finish together at the same moment in a strong, clear, accented endpoint. This endpoint establishes the rhythmicity of a Movement which is so essential in Fluid Strength. The rhythm and the accented endpoint are key to the strengthening and invigorating potential of the Movements.

Breathing in Fluid Strength has a bellows dynamic. Indeed it is taken from the "bellows" breath of yoga pranayama (bhastrika). Each Fluid Strength Movement functions like a bellows chamber in that it physically pushes the breath out of the body. The pressure of the movement and the pressure of the breath each energize the other which contributes greatly to the generation of functional strength.

Rib-Cage-Tap Breathing will help you to get a sense of this body/breath dynamic. The strong, springy pressure of the arms on the ribcage compresses the ribs and simulates the diaphragm. This creates the bellows-like pressure which intensifies the exhalation. Some Movements lend themselves easily to this breathing dynamic while in others it takes a little time to awaken. In Fluid Strength all breathing is done through the nose with the lips lightly sealed.

RIB-CAGE-TAP BREATHING

The diaphragm is our main breathing muscle. It can easily become stuck or restricted due to respiratory illness or mental and emotional stress. By freeing up the diaphragm, these movements facilitate full, whole body breathing. They enliven your body and restore a sense of well-being.

Rib-Cage-Tap Breathing will also give you a feel for how the movement of the body in Fluid Strength is used to strengthen the exhalation and intensify the breathing. The springy, vigorous pressure of the arms on the ribcage as you exhale directly simulates the diaphragm. This highlights the Fluid Strength dynamic that the Movements act like a bellows to push the breath out of the body.

⫷ RIB-CAGE-TAP BREATHING ~ FRONT ⫸

- Find a comfortable, well-supported seated position – sitting on a chair is fine
- Cross your arms in front of you and bring each hand to hold the opposite elbow
- Strongly tap your lower rib cage with your arms as if to push the breath out of the body
- Let the forearms spring away from the ribs on the inhale
- Alternate quickly and rhythmically between these two movements, maintaining a vigorous tap on the exhalation
- Stop

For videos of the Fluid Strength Movements – fluid-strength-yoga-practice.com

⫸ RIB-CAGE-TAP BREATHING ~ SIDE ⫷

- Bring your fingertips up to touch your collarbones
- Strongly tap the sides of the rib cage with your elbows on the exhale
- Let the elbows spring away from the ribs on the inhale
- Alternate quickly and rhythmically between these two movements, maintaining a vigorous tap on the exhalation
- Stop

⫸ RIB-CAGE-TAP BREATHING ~ BACK ⫷

- Bring your fingertips up to touch your collar bones
- Slide the shoulder blades toward the spine, bringing your elbows as far back as you can
- Strongly tap toward the ribcage with your elbows on the exhale
- Let the elbows spring away from the ribs on the inhale
- Alternate quickly and rhythmically between these two movements, maintaining a vigorous tap on the exhalation
- Stop

BELLOWS BREATH BENEFITS

Even a small improvement in how we breathe gives us significant benefits in physical strength, emotional balance, and mental clarity. Breath is one of our best resources for rejuvenation. In addition to the physical support the bellows breath provides the Fluid Strength Movements, it also provides all of the benefits ascribed to the bellows breath, including:

- Stimulating digestive fire
- Strengthening the lungs
- Cleansing the breathing passageways
- Calming and purifying the mind
- Strengthening and freeing the diaphragm
- Improving cardio-vascular function

BREATHING AND PRANA

Prana is the life force. It is a subtle energy that flows within the breath and throughout the body. Vibrant prana gives us a vibrant body and mind. Prana is nourishment and breathing is our easiest and most direct source of it.

Although related, prana and breath are different. Breath is restricted to the body. Prana can move together with the breath – and it can move separately, both through and around the body. We take in most of our prana through the breath, but we also take it in through food.

Pranic healers have developed their ability to gather and strengthen prana, and then use it to help fortify the weakened prana of someone who is ill, aged, or injured. In Fluid Strength we are fortifying our own prana.

Prana underlies all mental and physical activity. It supports our every action. When awakened and flowing freely, prana gives vitality and radiance to these activities. Our ability to heal, regenerate and transform is in direct proportion to our ability to balance, vitalize, and engage this energy.

STOPPING AND PRANA

Prana is powerfully stimulated by the energized body/breath interplay in the Fluid Strength Movements. Each Movement is then followed by conscious resting. This rest is referred to as Stopping. In it, our awareness opens into the space around our body and we sense the activated prana both within our body and in the space around it. This is referred to as Open Awareness.

The prana that we have awakened with a movement remains active for some time after the Movement is finished. In the expanded awareness of Stopping we rest within this enlivened prana and let it cleanse, nourish, and balance us. It can seem like a miracle when we sense prana moving directly in the areas where we most need help.

WHOLE-BODY AWARENESS

Every action we make, no matter how small, involves our whole self. This is true in the specific Movements of Fluid Strength and in all of the activities of our life. Some parts play an active role, while others play a supportive one. Being aware of the whole body in every Movement, regardless of its size, encourages all parts of ourselves to play their role effectively.

Your hand opens and closes
and opens and closes.
If it were always a fist or
always stretched open,
you would be paralyzed.
Your deepest presence is in every
small contracting and expanding,
the two as beautifully balanced
and coordinated as bird wings.
RUMI

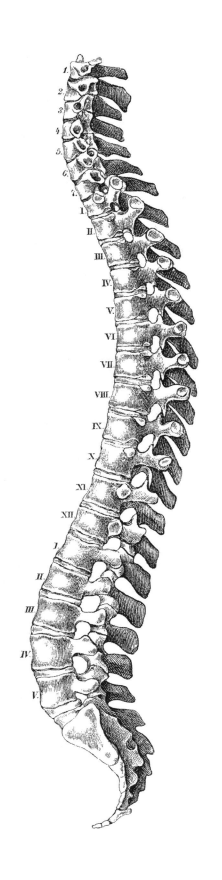

Spinal Flip

If you would seek health, look first to the spine. SOCRATES

A strong, mobile, and buoyant spine makes life more buoyant, and is a deep well of support for our well-being. When the spine is balanced the many muscles that attach to it are able to function easily and effectively, making life easier.

The spine and internal organs form the functional core of the body. A vital spine equals a strong body, a stable nervous system, and well-functioning tissues. It also gives us the confidence of "having a backbone."

Spinal Flip is the primary Movement in Fluid Strength. It mobilizes, strengthens, and enlivens the spine. Each practice begins with Spinal Flip in order to warm the body and awaken the midline. Each practice ends with a Spinal Flip as a way to harmonize the body, mind and breath. This Movement also serves as a reference to recognize improvements in strength and ease. Whole classes can be organized around discovering the potential of Spinal Flip for relieving pain, quieting the mind and integrating the whole body.

THREE LEVELS OF THE SPINE

Fluid Strength engages the spine on three different levels: the physical, the fluid and the energetic. The physical level is the *spinal column*, the fluid level is the *cerebrospinal fluid*, and the energetic level is the subtle channel within the spinal cord referred to in yoga anatomy as *sushumna*. Many people who do Fluid Strength report benefits touching on all three of these levels.

THE PHYSICAL SPINE

Returning the spinal column to its structural integrity is the concern of Chiropractic Medicine. The benefits include improving physical well-being, alleviating pain, and supporting the body's natural ability to renew itself. Well-aligned and mobile vertebrae allow for easy communication between the brain and the body, creating a good foundation for optimal health.

THE FLUID SPINE

The cerebrospinal fluid surrounds, nourishes, and protects the brain and spinal cord. In Biodynamic Craniosacral Therapy the cerebrospinal fluid is considered to be the most refined substance in the body and is said to carry the life-force (prana). The subtle, hands-on work of this therapy evokes remarkable healing by supporting free flow of the fluid spine.

THE ENERGETIC SPINE

An awakening of the spine is one way of describing the yogic goal of self-realization. We have a dormant life energy that lies sleeping at the base of the spine, and yoga seeks to rouse it. Once activated, this energy flows toward the head through the subtle channel within the spinal cord. On this upward journey, it opens the higher levels of consciousness that are associated with the seven chakras.

All three levels of the spine are engaged in the Spinal Flip Movement. Its lively alternating flexions and extensions remove kinks from the spinal column and help it return to alignment. The massaging pulsations created through Spinal Flip encourage a release of restrictions in the tissue around the fluid spine which support its balanced flow. Resting into and relying on the rhythm of Spinal Flip to carry the movement is a gentle surrender to the life within us. This combination of balancing the physical spine, freeing the flow of the fluid spine, and yielding into the support of rhythm is a three-fold boost for our health, wellness and our personal development.

AWAKENING THE SPINE

The Spinal Flip Movement is done while lying on your back with feet flat on the floor. The legs are held together to form a stabilizing midline. A dynamic, rhythmic, wave-like motion is created in the torso by alternating flexion and

A man is as young as his spinal column.
JOSEPH PILATES

extension movements of the spine. When the lower back is lifted away from the floor, the back of the neck is pressing into the floor. When the lower back is pressing into the floor, the neck is arching away from it. We are looking to allow a synchronous rolling of the pelvis and head.

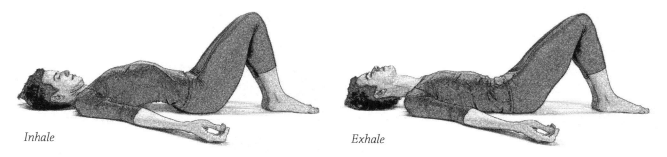

Inhale   *Exhale*

If we "try" to do Spinal Flip it usually eludes us. It is a natural movement that we are seeking to uncover, rather than something we have to figure out. We find it most easily through an attitude of play and exploration.

Spinal Flip simultaneously cultivates differentiated movement between each vertebra and integrates the whole spine. The breath infused rhythmicity of the Movement enlivens the spine and taps into its potential for stimulating health on all three levels. The Movement is described in full on page 96.

ENERGIZED BODY AND BREATH

The rhythmic, alternating wave-like flexions and extensions of the spine in Spinal Flip are infused with and vitalized by the breath. The exhale happens when the lower back is pressed into the floor and the inhale happens when the lower back is arched away from the floor.

This body/breath merging uses the breath to create vitality in the body and uses the body to clarify and strengthen the breath. The result is that they are both developed simultaneously.

The body and breath press into each other throughout the Movement. An ideal Movement is one that feels equally as if the breath is moving the body and the body is moving the breath. This strong and intimate body/breath interplay reestablishes a healthy responsiveness between our breath and our body.

HEALTH AND FLUID STRENGTH

A vital, mobile core is essential to the Fluid Strength view of health. This includes well-functioning organs; a strong, springy spine; and free, balanced flow of body fluids and nerve energy.

HEALTHY ORGANS

The alternating flexion and extension of Spinal Flip creates a deep, rippling pulsation along the spine. Each pulsation pushes, pulls, squeezes, and releases the internal organs in a health-stimulating massage.

This massage encourages the inherent movement in each of the organs, which is essential for them to function well. It also awakens the deep, simple pleasure of being alive.

SPRINGY SPINE

On a skeletal level, the bony vertebrae alternate with soft discs to give us the full range of motion in our spine. Spinal Flip pumps fluid into the discs which keeps them moist and doing their job effectively. Some of our loss in height as we age is that the discs lose their moisture and plumpness. When the discs become dry our spinal column settles and our movement suffers.

Spinal Flip helps the spine maintain its full height. It vitalizes the springy, accordion-like movement potential in this bone-disc interplay and gives us a strong, flexible midline.

FLOW IS HEALTH

Balanced, unobstructed flow of life energy through our body/mind is traditional medicine's definition of health. When flow is balanced, when it is not too little or too much, our well-being is assured. The image of the flow of life-energy through our whole self can be a powerful daily inspiration for helping us create our greatest health and highest happiness.

Spinal Flip cultivates a vital, balanced flow through the spine and is one of our best friends on our journey to this health and happiness.

> Learn to let go and allow the changing mystery of life to move through you without fearing it, without holding or grasping.
> JACK KORNFIELD

Resting

Through **Transitional Awareness,** we access a calm mind and four progressively more subtle levels of our inner world. We use this process to start a practice.

The essentialness of learning how to rest deeply and trust the life within us is highlighted in the chapter on **Stopping**.

In **We Need Wisdom,** we are reminded of the importance of touching into what truly makes life meaningful.

Koyasan, Japan

Transitional Awareness

Accepting means you allow yourself to feel whatever it is you are feeling at that moment. It is part of the isness of the Now. You can't argue with what is. Well, you can, but if you do, you suffer. ECKHART TOLLE

Being present to each moment is where yoga begins. As such, each Fluid Strength practice starts with Transitional Awareness, a four-part process to come to this presence.

In taking care of the details of daily living we can lose touch with ourselves. Transitional Awareness is a time for connecting to and acknowledging what is happening inside you.

It is done lying on the back in a position that closely resembles the corpse pose (savasana). The two slight differences are the palms are facing the side body rather than facing upward; and the legs are slightly closer together than they usually are in savasana.

Transitional Awareness brings a heightened connection to yourself as you start a practice. With an attitude of complete acceptance, you invite your whole self to be present. This includes the parts of yourself that you are consciously aware of and the parts of yourself that are in your unconscious. It includes the parts of yourself that you like and the parts with which you are uncomfortable. It is full receptivity to everything that you were in the past, are in the present and will become in the future.

This process releases physical tension, calms the mind, and opens you to yourself in a way that supports getting the maximum benefit from your practice.

> **The four phases of Transitional Awareness are:**
>
> **Honor** | **Sense** | **Open** | **Receive**

Each phase progresses naturally from the previous one. Once you have become familiar with them as a progression, it is beneficial to use them individually in order to more fully develop them.

PRACTICING TRANSITIONAL AWARENESS

To start this practice, lie on your back with arms resting easily beside you with palms facing toward the body. Then:

≫ HONOR ≪

Become present to what is active in you physically, mentally, and/or emotionally. Whatever is there, simply be present to it – without engaging with its story line. There might be physical pain, mental agitation, or emotional disturbance. On the other hand you might be feeling very excited or happy, confident or content. Nothing is judged either negatively or positively. You are simply cultivating the ability to be calm and accepting of whatever is happening in you in the moment.

≫ SENSE ≪

After honoring what is active in you, gently shift your attention to your whole body. Move your consciousness into and through your body's entire length, width, and depth, from the top of your head to the tips of your feet and hands. Sense your body in its entirety.

As you are sensing your whole self, maintain that awareness while noticing the subtle sensations occurring in your body. These sensations will be ebbing and flowing moment by moment. They are arising from the softening that happens as your body settles into the floor, from the movement of your breathing, and from all the other movements of life happening inside you. Movement creates sensations, and no matter how externally still, a living body is in endless motion. In this phase you are learning to perceive these subtle sensations.

≫ OPEN ≪

Continuing to sense your whole self, let your awareness soften and expand into the field around you. This expanding of awareness, called Open Awareness, is similar to opening your eyes into peripheral vision. If you are standing on a mountain and want to take in the whole vista you need only to soften your eyes and presto – you are in peripheral vision. It is a natural and easy thing to do. Opening your awareness into the field around your body is natural in this same way.

Resting in Open Awareness softens our whole being and gives us a more expansive sense of self. It can be profoundly peaceful.

≫ RECEIVE ≪

Open Awareness and receiving are interconnected. They happen almost simultaneously. Once you have opened your awareness into the space around your body, you rest in it with an easy, comfortable receptivity.

There is nothing special that you need to receive; you are simply cultivating the physical, mental, and emotional attitude of receiving. If it is more comfortable for you to think of receiving something, you can receive peace, contentment, light, healing, energy, or safety.

As you cultivate an attitude of receiving, the body lets go of tension and the natural pleasure of being alive emerges. This attitude of receiving awakens gentleness, supports self-kindness, and encourages tranquility.

....

Transitional Awareness can be used in different ways. It can be done in a few minutes to just brush off the dust of the day. If you are tired or stressed, taking five to eight minutes with it can smooth your way into a practice. Doing it for twenty minutes without continuing on into the Movements can make a nice restorative practice. I highly recommend deepening your experience of the individual phases by periodically devoting five to ten minutes to each one, either before a practice or on its own.

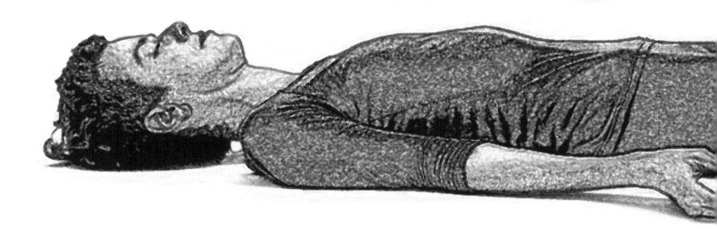

HONOR

Become present to
what is active in you
physically, mentally,
and/or emotionally.

thinking
over
a to do list

feeling of
impatience

sensations
of lower back
pain

SENSE

Once you have sense of your body as a whole,
begin to notice the subtle changing sensations
that happen within moment by moment

> Yoga practice can make us more and more sensitive to subtler and subtler sensations in the body. Paying attention to and staying with finer and finer sensations within the body is one of the surest ways to steady the wandering mind.
>
> RAVI RAVINDRA,
> THE WISDOM OF PATANJALI'S YOGA SUTRAS

old memories arising

left leg heavier than right

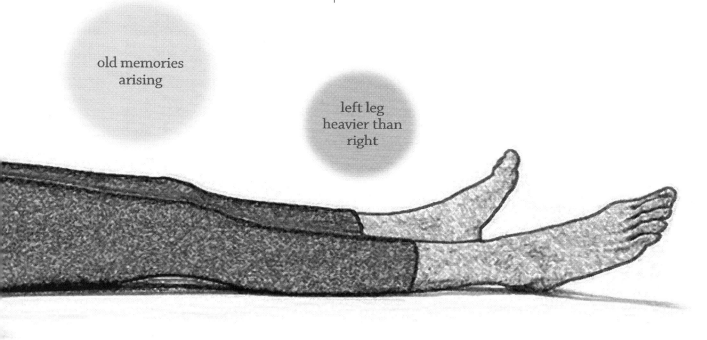

OPEN

Become aware of the field around your body. Allow the sensation of your body to recede and the sensation of the field to become more prominent.

RECEIVE

Cultivate the sensation of receptivity by imagining your body becoming more permeable – invite the pores of your skin and the cells of your body to open and receive the presence of the field.

Awaken to the mystery
of being here
And enter the quiet
immensity
of your own presence.
JOHN O'DONOHUE

Stopping

Our fast-paced culture makes it difficult to stay connected to ourselves and our needs. The cost of this to our well-being is high.

Learning to stop can be profound. It gives our body and mind a chance to regain equilibrium. It gives us the space to remember that our life is in the present moment. Building stops into our day makes it less likely that we will be forced to stop by collapsing from overwork or by getting sick.

We are stopped many times during our day in grocery lines, at stoplights, and being on hold. With a little mind shift we can change our impatience into gratitude and use those moments to push the refresh button.

SPURTING AND STOPPING IN FLUID STRENGTH

Every Fluid Strength Movement finishes with Spurting and Stopping. Right before the Movement ends the mind and body are concentrated more deeply by *spurting*, bringing the Movement up to full speed. It is a similar dynamic to an athlete spurting near a finish line. Spurting increases the stimulation of prana and helps us to maintain a no-thought mind through the transition from moving into Stopping. Spurting is a change in the dynamic of the Movement and sometimes makes the Movement easier and clearer. Because spurting is a full-on transitional action it is done for a short period of time – less than a minute.

Stopping in Fluid Strength is a full stop. We are cultivating a still body, a thought-free mind, spacious awareness, and an attitude of surrender. It is done in the same position as Transitional Awareness, and it also uses its third and fourth phases: Open and Receive (see Open on page 59).

Empty your mind
of all thoughts.
let your heart
be at peace
LAO-TZU

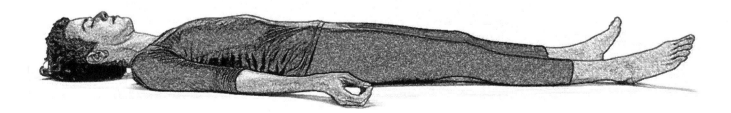

Every Fluid Strength Movement is following by Stopping. Stopping is usually done lying on your back with arms alongside your body, with your legs extended. The knees can be bent with feet standing on the floor if extending the legs creates discomfort. Stopping lasts for one to three minutes.

Although Stopping mirrors the corpse pose in yoga, it has a slightly different focus. Rather than a relaxation with its progression of releasing each part of the body, Stopping focuses on cultivating an expansive, receptive awareness that extends into the space around the body, and on releasing the body as a whole.

While muscles do relax in this process, it is not the goal. The goal is to access a soft, Open Awareness that extends beyond the surface of the body and to rest fully and easily in the present moment. The focus is on sensing your whole self in suspension and surrender. It is an experience very similar to that of floating in water or the awe of being "stopped" by beauty.

STOPPING AND OPEN AWARENESS

Every living being is surrounded by and permeated with an energy field. It is called by different names such as the auric field, chi field, or morphogenetic field. In yoga it is referred to as the pranic field.

Prana is life energy that underlies and organizes all of the functions in our body. Energy healers can create remarkable therapeutic results without ever touching the body simply by working with this field. It is a very real thing. In becoming aware of our own pranic field, we are developing a powerful resource for our own personal and spiritual growth.

In Fluid Strength, the moment we stop moving, we extend the arms and legs and open our awareness into this field. This is referred to as Open Awareness (and is also the 3rd phase of Transitional Awareness). Opening into this field is as natural as adjusting our eyes from the focused vision of reading a book, to peripheral vision in order to take in a vista.

Developing the ability to move easily into and out of peripheral vision and peripheral awareness helps keep our mind, body, and senses flexible and balanced. It also increases our sense of connection to life.

RESTING IN PRANA

The Fluid Strength Movements enliven prana. When a Movement stops, prana remains active for a period of time. While resting in Open Awareness we can sense enlivened energy flowing through our body and in the field around it.

It is important to keep a thought-free mind when transitioning from moving to Stopping; the activated prana supports that happening. Thinking keeps our focus narrow, making it impossible to sustain Open Awareness. Thinking also uses a lot of energy, which means it uses a lot of prana. The result is to reduce the amount of time that this energy remains active.

Open Awareness and a thought-free mind allow prana to remain active for a longer period of time, giving us more access to its power for stimulating deep healing and awakening spontaneous meditation.

Prana is life's healing energy. Resting in Open Awareness allows this energy to flow freely through the body and go to the places in us where it is most needed.

People experience enlivened prana differently, and each Movement tends to stimulate it differently. It is, however, surprising easy for most people to sense this life energy and its movement.

Resting in prana is a tool for self-transformation. In it we develop our capacity to trust and surrender. Our self-image expands as we recognize our energy body as a part of who we are. We have the chance to savor and be renewed by the power of Stopping and stillness.

BAHMAN FARZAD

I wish I could show you One day
When you are lonely or in darkness,
The Astonishing Light
Of your own Being!
HAFIZ

We Need Wisdom

We are a culture that is glutted with information and starved for wisdom. Huge amounts of information pour through our mind, body, and senses each day, without enhancing our lives. Conversely, if we allow ourselves to absorb even a tiny bit of wisdom, it can transform us.

Yoga and Ayurveda are wisdom traditions. Wisdom principles speak to us of our highest potential, orient us toward what truly matters, and provide guidance for how to live a good life.

WISDOM IN FLUID STRENGTH

Wisdom principles are integrated into every Fluid Strength class. This is done with a short quote that is read a number of times during the Stopping phase, such as "Life begins where fear ends" (Osho). In Stopping, the mind is soft, open and receptive, an ideal state for absorbing a new idea and helping its meaning to take root.

Rather than thinking about the meaning of what is being read, students are encouraged to allow the quote to simply flow through their body and mind; being present to the words and their meaning, but not actively thinking about them. The quote is put on a small piece of paper along with an image and given to students at the end of class.

It has been heartwarming for me to hear about some of the ways students use these little pieces of paper. They organize them in books, pass them along to a friend, tape them on a wall, or stack them on their desk. People talk about how remembering a quote helps them to respond differently in difficult situations. I see people's eyes full with emotion as they tell me their experience of feeling that a quote was read "just for them."

It gives me optimism to realize what a beautiful difference a few words of wisdom can make. A couple of minutes spent absorbing their meaning can warm and soften our lives. Wisdom wants to grow in us; we just need to give it a little help.

When practicing alone, choose a wisdom quote that is short so you can easily remember it. During stopping, allow it to arise in you, being aware of it but giving it no special attention. Sensing it flow through the body with prana is helpful for some people. There are many quotes throughout this book that you can use. Having a book of short quotes is a good resource.

Wisdom is our access into harmonizing ourselves with life.

As wisdom grows, we...

... become clear on what is important to us.

... see the larger picture of life which helps us see more options and feel less trapped by difficult situations.

... remain calm in facing the challenges and uncertainties of life.

... grow more love, tolerance, self-understanding, and compassion.

... more easily stay on track with that which fulfills us.

... live more skillfully and wholeheartedly with ourselves and others.

... come into alignment with the universe and recognize that we are connected to everything within it.

... reduce the friction in our lives, discover more of our potential, and invite the spontaneous arising of happiness.

... flow more easily with the ups and downs of life.

... make better decisions, live with integrity, and tap into our capacity for joy.

... navigate the journey of life with grace.

... become confident in knowing that we can face and solve life's problems.

The "bubbles" list benefits that can themselves be used as thoughts to contemplate.

Empowering the Movements

This section talks about two aspects of the Fluid Strength Yoga Practice that are specifically for cultivating strength and skill in the Movements. *The Midline and Mermaid Legs* discusses the benefits of a clear midline and offers awareness meditations for accessing this clarity.

Four Qualities are used to refine the Fluid Strength Movements. The greatest benefit of this practice comes through awakening these qualities.

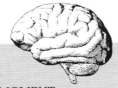

Working with Imbalances

When working with imbalance of strength in the two sides of the body, our impulse is to focus on strengthening the weaker side. It is more effective to reduce the work of the stronger side until the two sides are evenly matched and then strengthen them both together.

This is also true if one side is more mobile than the other. Rather than trying to move the less mobile side as much as the more mobile side, it is more effective to reduce the more mobile side to match the less mobile side and then challenge their range of movement together.

Each side of the body relies on the other side. If we overlook this functional relationship and treat the two sides as separate, we work against ourselves.

Midline and Mermaid Legs

Cultivating a strong, clear midline is a major goal in Fluid Strength.

The midline is the vertical center of the body. The spine is its most obvious expression, but it has a number of increasingly subtle layers. It is via the midline that our left and right sides relate to each other. It literally holds us together.

The midline also extends energetically beyond the tailbone and above the crown of the head, serving as the axis through which we connect to heaven and earth.

When we have a reliable sense of our midline, everything we do requires less effort. It gives strength to our limbs, ease to our breathing and is the basis of a harmonious relationship between the two sides of our body. When both sides of the body relate easily to the midline, our whole system is in balance.

A strong, vital, clear midline brings physical integrity and a steady mind. It is an ever-available resource for us in regaining equilibrium on all all levels.

SOLAR AND LUNAR

In yoga anatomy, the two sides of the body represent life's polar energies. The right side is the solar, masculine energy. It is active and heating. The left side is the lunar, feminine energy. It is receptive and cooling. This polarity is beautifully expressed in 'hatha' yoga, with 'ha' meaning sun and 'tha' meaning moon.

A familiar symbol for balancing these opposites is the gesture of 'namaste,' the prayer position. Bringing the palms together at the midline symbolizes the merging of the masculine and feminine energies. In doing this we come to our center and connect to our source. Balancing these energies balances our life.

Mermaid Legs is sometimes referred to as Namaste Legs because it mirrors the namaste prayer position of the hands.

> Each one of us needs to discover the proper balance between the masculine and feminine energies, between the active and the receptive.
> RAVI RAVINDRA, THE WISDOM OF PATANJALI'S YOGA SUTRAS

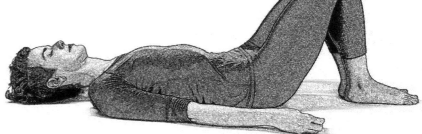

MERMAID LEGS AND THE MIDLINE

Mermaid Legs is the primary means of engaging the midline in the Fluid Strength Movements. Mermaid Legs is simply bringing the inner legs in contact with each other in order to awaken and strengthen the presence of the midline. It is used in every Fluid Strength Movement (page 94).

Most Fluid Strength Movements are done lying on our back with knees bent and feet flat on the floor. In this position, Mermaid Legs connects the legs along the inside edges of the feet, knees, and thighs. Maintaining the legs in this way steadies the body and orients us to our vertical center. It gathers our strength to support the midline and vigorous movement of the torso.

There are some Movements in which the legs are not symmetrical or fully drawn together, but even then the *energetic* relationship of Mermaid Legs is maintained in order to stay connected to the midline.

MIDLINE IMBALANCES

There are two common ways that we lose access to the full support of our midline by holding on to it – or losing connection to it.

We may have developed a habit of gripping the spine in an effort to feel safe and physically stable. This creates hardness along the midline which makes breathing difficult and limits ease of movement. It causes brittleness in the spine which can extend throughout the whole body.

Although the midline never goes away, we can lose our connection to it. This leaves the two sides of the body relating to each other without a stabilizing center. We become physically unsteady, which increases the amount of energy and effort we need to move our body. Physical activity is easier when we are connected to our center.

Strengthening and vitalizing the midline is a major focus in Fluid Strength. The following Midline Meditations can be used to help us reconnect with the midline. They also can be used to help us release our grip on the spine.

MIDLINE MEDITATIONS FOR CLARIFYING THE MIDLINE

The following meditations can be used to get in touch with the midline. The awareness you gain from doing these meditations can then be brought into the Fluid Strength Movements to help strengthen and clarify them. Doing this further awakens the midline. In this way the muscles and organs are given support for regaining a functional relationship with the midline and spine.

The exercises can be done either sitting or lying. Use any support that helps you to hold the spine in an easy elongation and maintain its natural curves. It is beneficial to do the same meditation both sitting up and lying because each position evokes a slightly different experience of the midline. Before beginning, take time to quiet your system and awaken whole body presence. You can use the Transitional Awareness (page 57) practice or any other quieting process that you are familiar with.

⫸ DRAWING A MENTAL MIDLINE ⫷

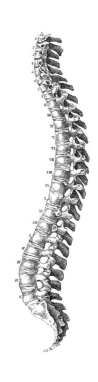

- Establish internal quiet and whole-body awareness.

- Use your mind like a laser pen to slowly draw a fine thin line along the length of the spine. Start at the tip of the tailbone and end at the top of the spine at the level of the point between the eyes.

- Repeat this 5 to 8 times, resting for a minute between each drawing.

⫸ MIDLINE AS A SHAFT OF LIGHT ⫷

- Establish internal quiet and whole-body awareness.

- Use your mind's eye to create a beam of light starting from below the tailbone running up along the spine and extending a foot or more above the crown of the head.

- Once you have established this light, rest quietly with it and the sense that it is supporting you. Rest and maintain it for up to 5 minutes.

⫸ MIDLINE AS EMPTINESS ⫷

- Establish internal quiet and whole-body awareness.

- Bring your attention deep into the spinal cord and evoke the presence of a thin empty tube within the cord from the tailbone and ending in the middle of the brain.

- Once the tube is present to you rest quietly for 5 minutes or more with a simultaneous awareness of the tube and your relaxed breathing.

⫸ THE FLUID MIDLINE ⫷

- Establish internal quiet and whole-body awareness.

- The brain and the spinal cord are protected by cerebrospinal fluid. Become aware of the brain and cord being suspended in this fluid support. Keep reawakening the sensation of the brain and cord floating.

- Rest in this fluid midline for up to 20 minutes.

The Midline Meditations center us very quickly and can be used within a practice or throughout our day. Some people have an easier time than others being aware of the midline. If it is not so easy for you, finding a favorite meditation and using it throughout the day can help you awaken your midline. Doing a meditation for just one or two minutes when you go to bed can clarify your midline and help you sleep. Doing one just before getting out of bed can help you to start the day feeling centered. The midline is more easily available in some Fluid Strength Movements than in others. In a challenging Movement you can pause for a minute and use a Meditation to access midline support.

Another important aspect is that the masters taught us to move from a deeper source, not just from muscles and joints.
T. K.V. DESIKACHAR

The Four Qualities of Movement

It is through qualities that we can most easily describe that which enriches us: the layered depth in the color of a sunset, the contrast and harmony of flavors in a skillfully prepared meal, the dense, moist sweetness of spring air.

All of our actions, experiences and communications are imbued with qualities. The simple act of setting a table can be done with reverence or irritation. Facing a challenge can be done with pleasure or resentment. In both cases, the table will be set and the challenge will be met. Whether we are enriched or diminished by the activity depends primarily on the qualities with which it is done. The setting of the table or the facing of the challenge is a *container*, and the qualities of mind, emotions, and actions with which they are done is the *content*.

The words "I love you" can be said with soft tenderness, strong passion, playful humor, sharp sarcasm, cold anger or whiny neediness. The words are the same but what is being expressed is very different. It is through the qualities that we know the truth and meaning of any action, experience, or communication.

70% OF THE BENEFIT!

Vitality, health, and a responsive body all have particular qualities. We recognize and are attracted to people who have these qualities. They remind us, in some deep way, that at some point we ourselves possessed them, that they are natural and they are "right".

In doing the Fluid Strength Movements, we bring qualities of aliveness to the forefront of our awareness. A Movement is a *container* and health-generating qualities are the *content*. By awakening these qualities we are helping ourselves to remember easy, pleasurable and vital movement. We are using movement to prime the pump of our health and aliveness.

> We don't move ourselves through telling certain muscles to lengthen or shorten, but through our images of movement.
> BONNIE ANGELIE

70% of the benefit of a Movement comes from infusing it with qualities – *even if our movement barely resembles the actual Fluid Strength Movement we are trying to do.*

This focus on cultivating qualities is a paradigm shift from the usual ways of working with the body. We need to reinforce this notion many times in order for it to sink in: ***Cultivating qualities is 70% of this practice.***

THE FOUR FLUID STRENGTH QUALITIES

Fluid Strength focuses on four Qualities. These qualities are present in all comfortable, skillful, and efficient movement. They are:

Light	**Springy**	**Rhythmic**	**Reflexive**

These Qualities are seen most easily in babies, children, and highly skilled adults. The movements of babies and children are especially light and springy. The movements of highly skilled adults have a deep rhythmicity and well-integrated reflexes.

As a child, our body knew these Qualities. In the Fluid Strength Movements, we are helping it to remember them. These Movements are simple and repetitive and so are ideal for cultivating qualities. Once a Movement has been initiated, very little attention is needed to sustain it. This frees us to focus on awakening the Qualities.

For videos of the Fluid Strength Movements – fluid-strength-yoga-practice.com

LIGHT

A light movement is free from unnecessary effort. How much effort we use in moving our body is deeply habitual and mostly out of conscious control. Bringing it into our awareness is the first step in being able to reduce it.

To cultivate light movement we need to let go of excess effort and parasitic actions. Excess effort is simply working harder than an activity requires. Parasitic actions are created by using muscles that, rather than helping us to do a movement, actually work against it.

Fluid Strength uses awareness of the skeleton to help in cultivating lightness of movement. The skeleton is the simplest and clearest route through the body. It acts as a sort of freeway. When we move through the skeleton, the muscles have support for releasing excess effort.

Walking, page 122

≫ EXPLORING LIGHTNESS ≪

Walking lends itself well to exploring lightness, as does **Arm Slide**.

Let the movement go through the skeleton rather than the muscles. Go back and forth a number of times between moving through the muscles and moving through the skeleton in order to identify the difference. Sense the heaviness in muscle dominant movement, and the lightness in the skeletal dominant movement. Keep exploring and thinking skeleton.

While doing the Movement keep reducing the amount of effort you are using by half – and then again by half – without changing the size or speed of the movement. Learning to use less effort and finding lightness is truly a gift.

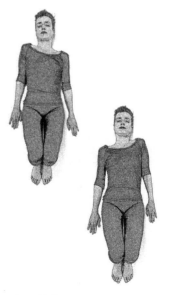

Arm Slide, page 108

SPRINGY

Springiness is the ability to bounce back. This capacity to rebound, physically, and mentally and emotionally, is the key to gracefully navigating life's challenges.

Springiness is an enhanced form of flexibility. Flexibility is about lengthening muscles and increasing the range of motion in joints. In addition to freeing muscles and mobilizing joints, the springy quality in Fluid Strength develops rebound and resiliency. In developing spring we are also encouraging responsive breathing and whole-body integration.

Cultivating physical springiness primes us for mental and emotional springiness. It helps us to bounce back more readily on all three levels.

Belly Pump, page 104

≫ EXPLORING SPRINGINESS ≪

Belly Pump and **SI Tap** are good Movements for exploring springiness. The Belly Pump has a softer, looser spring quality, while the SI Tap has a smaller, tighter spring quality.

Springs come in all sizes, weights and tensions. The more variety of springiness we create in our movements, the more freedom, ease and responsiveness we will awaken in our body. Vitalize the springiness and experiment with different amounts of tension. Invite your whole body to participate in the spring of the movement, even with the smaller spring of SI Tap.

SI Tap, page 100

RHYTHMIC

Our life is sustained by rhythm – the beating heart, the inhale and exhale, the ebbing and flowing of fluids and the pumping of peristalsis. We are polyrhythmic beings.

These rhythms are mostly unconscious, but we can consciously use rhythm to great benefit. Finding a rhythm in daily chores makes them easier and more pleasurable. Losing ourselves in rhythm gives us a taste of its power to heal. Rhythm is the foundation of all skillful and pleasurable physical activity.

Rhythm is the ground of every Fluid Strength Movement. We establish a strong body/breath rhythm, and then allow that rhythm to sustain the Movement. Letting ourselves yield into the support of that rhythm as we move, deeply harmonizes our body and mind.

Spinal Flip, page 96

≫ EXPLORING RHYTHMICITY ≪

Spinal Flip is a good Movement for finding rhythmicity, so also is **Shoulder Figure 8**.

Find the rhythm in the center of the body in both of these Movements. Even though the primary action in Shoulder Figure 8 is in the upper back and shoulder girdle, the feeling of rhythm is in the deep center of the body.

Explore different rhythms, looking for ones with which you feel most natural and at home. Different rhythms will change the size and dynamics of the Movement.

Shoulder Figure 8, page 110

REFLEXIVE

All of our movement is organized through reflexes. Within every physical action are multiple layers of integrated reflexes. They are the unconscious support that we rely on in everything we do. Well-integrated reflexes give us refined, elegant movement and make physical activity a pleasure. Without them, we lack coordination and grace.

We cannot practice reflexes per se, but we can create situations to stimulate and integrate them. In Fluid Strength we are not engaging individual reflexes, but rather awakening a reflexive quality in movement. This tones our reflexes and keeps them responsive. Like all body functions, if we attend to them, they stay healthy.

Clamshell, page 112

Wood Chop, page 106

⫸ EXPLORING REFLEXIVITY ⫷

Clamshell and **Woodchop** are good options for exploring reflexivity.

Bring to mind a doctor tapping your knee with a rubber mallet to test your reflexes. If the reflex is healthy, your lower leg snaps upward. In cultivating reflexivity we are looking to mimic this quality.

The reflexive quality happens as a clear, staccato movement with a strong, definite end-point. In Clamshell, awaken the reflexive quality of the lower-leg-snap at the end of the exhale movement. The exhale movement in both Clamshell and Woodchop are simple and direct with distinct, firm finishes.

All skillful body use, whether in the Fluid Strength Movements or in daily life, has lightness, springiness, rhythmicity, and reflexiveness. Different actions will have a predominance of one or more of them. Since we use our body in everything we do, cultivating these qualities will make everything we do a little easier.

You may enjoy getting to know qualities outside of the Movements themselves:

- When people-watching, look for the presence or absence of light, springy, rhythmic and reflexive qualities in their movement.
- Similarly, look for these qualities in the movements of animals.
- Explore YouTube for examples of the four qualities in dancers, athletes, and children. Particularly, look for martial artists. They offer magnificent examples, particularly of lightness and reflexiveness.

The deepest words of the wise man teach us
the same as the whistle of the wind when it blows
or the sound of the water when it is flowing.
ANTONIO MACHADO

PART 2

Practicing

You have to learn how to listen
to your body, going with it and
not against it, avoiding all effort
or strain… You will be amazed to
discover that, if you are kind to
your body, it will respond in
an incredible way.
VANDA SCARAVELLI

The Fluid Strength Movements

This section gives you images and clear instructions for each of the Movements.

The **Practice Structure** is a visual outline for easy reference to the different steps that make up this practice; while **Wisdom Words** gives you a selection of short quotes that you can use for enhancing it. Learning to reduce effort in the Movements is a central theme in Fluid Strength. This theme is highlighted in the **Neuro Moment: Trying Less**.

The bulk of this section is given to descriptions of all of the Movements with step-by-step instructions for doing them, along with supportive information for refining them. The **Practice Points** will enhance the Movement with which they appear, but all of the Points are applicable to all of the Movements.

Note the **small image** of the Movement in the upper corner of the right page. It is a handy tool for flipping through the corners of the pages to find a particular Movement.

Each Movement tends to have a **dominant quality** which is included in the Movement information below the images. Remember, however, that all four qualities are present to some degree in every movement.

For *Videos* of the Fluid Strength Movements ~

fluid-strength-yoga-practice.com

Practice Structure Step by Step

❀ CHOOSE WISDOM WORDS

Infuse your practice with **wisdom** ~ *See next page.*

❀ TRANSITIONAL AWARENESS

Each practice **starts** with **Transitional Awareness.**

In-depth text on page 57

❀ MERMAID LEGS

Each Movement **starts** with **Mermaid Legs.**

In-depth text on page 73

❀ MOVEMENTS

The **Movements** last for 2-4 minutes or until you are pleasantly fatigued.

See Movement Index for overview of Movements, page 139

❀ SPURT

A Spurt **smooths** the **transition** into Stopping.

In-depth text on page 63

❀ STOP

Each Movement is **followed** by **Stopping** which lasts from 1-3 minutes.

Remember that a Movement and Stopping are two sides of one coin.

In-depth text on page 63

❀ OPEN AWARENESS

Stopping **includes** Open Awareness.

In-depth text on page 64

REMEMBER:

Four Qualities
(page 77)

Breath
(page 42)

Wisdom Words

It is not essential to use a wisdom principle during a practice, but it does add another layer of richness. You can have a wonderful practice without one.

The following quotes are short and have a simple, clear message. Don't try to memorize the words, just get the idea/feeling of them.

Let the idea/feeling arise as a *flavor* in Stopping, not as a *clear thought*.

The quality of awareness in Stopping is similar to the half-sleep state just before going to sleep, and just after awakening. The dreamlike way that images, thoughts and feelings happen in us during that state is similar to how we want the wisdom quotes to arise in us during Stopping.

Rest in natural great peace.
NYOSHUL KHEN RINPOCHE

❀

Keeping your body healthy
is an expression of gratitude
to the whole cosmos.
THICH NHAT HANH

❀

Meditate more and more
on what corresponds to
the innermost longing
of your heart.
YOGA SUTRAS: TRANSLATED
BY RAVI RAVINDRA

❀

Do not ask for less
responsibility to be free
and relaxed – ask for
more strength!
SHENGYAN

❀

Never hurry
through the world
But walk slowly,
and bow often.
MARY OLIVER

❀

❀

Peace and stillness are the
great remedy for disease.
When we can bring peace
into our cells, we are cured.
THE MOTHER

❀

We need for the earth
to sing through our pores
and eyes.
HAFIZ

❀

It makes a wonderful
difference whether we
find in the body an ally
or an adversary.
GOETHE

❀

I exist as I am,
that is enough.
WALT WHITMAN

❀

May your body be blessed.
May you realize that
your body is a
faithful and beautiful
friend of your soul.
JOHN O'DONOHUE

❀

One day you will wake up
and there won't be any
more time to do the things
you've always wanted to
do. Do them now.
PAULO COELHO

❀

Today I will open the
door of my calmness
and let the footsteps of
Silence gently enter the
temple of all my activities.
PARMAMHANSA YOGANANADA

❀

Never underestimate
the absolute importance –
and the difficulty –
of starting each encounter
with a primal "yes!"
RICHARD ROHR

❀

And you too have come
into the world to do this,
to go easy, to be filled
with light, and to shine.
MARY OLIVER

❀

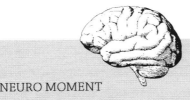

NEURO MOMENT

Trying Less

When we find a Movement difficult, we tend to try harder. We muster determination, intensify our focus and increase our effort. Although it feels like this will help, what we are actually doing is reinforcing that which is not working.

By decreasing effort, we become more sensitive to *how* we are doing the Movement, which is the doorway into seeing possibilities for improving it. If we don't know how we are doing a movement, we have no way of knowing how to do it differently, and so we will continue to do the same thing. Without awareness, we must rely on unconscious habits. In listening to the sensory information being communicated by the body, we are developing the awareness we need to discover easier and more comfortable ways of moving.

Although it is counterintuitive, when we feel challenged and the impulse to *try harder* arises, we must respond by *working less*. This will give us the greatest improvement in the shortest period of time. It is working smarter, not harder.

Transitional Awareness

PRACTICE POINTS

- Cultivate whole body presence.

- Invite a sense of permeability in the body.

- The field surrounds your whole body – front, back, both sides, below your feet and above your head.

TRANSITIONAL AWARENESS
Step-by-Step

Transitional Awareness is a process for coming fully into the present moment.

- **Honor** - Notice what is most active in you in the moment, honoring it without judging it negative or positive

- **Sense** - Receive the sensation of your whole body in its entirety

- **Open** - Expand your awareness into the field around your body

- **Receive** - Cultivate a sensation of receptivity in the body as if receiving energy from the field

NOTE

Transitional Awareness is done at the beginning of a practice;

Stopping is done between each Movement.

 TEXT ON
57

Mermaid Legs

PRACTICE POINTS

- Find a sense of quiet in the midline and let that quiet support you.

- Enliven the midline by remembering one of the Midline Meditations (page 75).

- Soften the outer body and vitalize the spine.

NOTE

"Magnetized" describes the attraction of the legs toward each other and creates a more integrated action of the legs. It helps get away from the muscular effort of "holding" the legs together.

MERMAID LEGS Step-by-Step

- Bend your legs and bring your feet flat on the floor

- Rotate your thighs inward as you press the inner ankles, knees and thighs into each other

- Allow the legs to come together as if magnetized

- Strongly, sensitively merge the legs, rather than holding them together muscularly

- Enliven the soles of your feet

- Maintain a soft receptivity in the lower belly

- Sense the skin of your inner thighs and encourage it to flow upward toward the pelvis

TEXT ON
73

Mermaid Legs

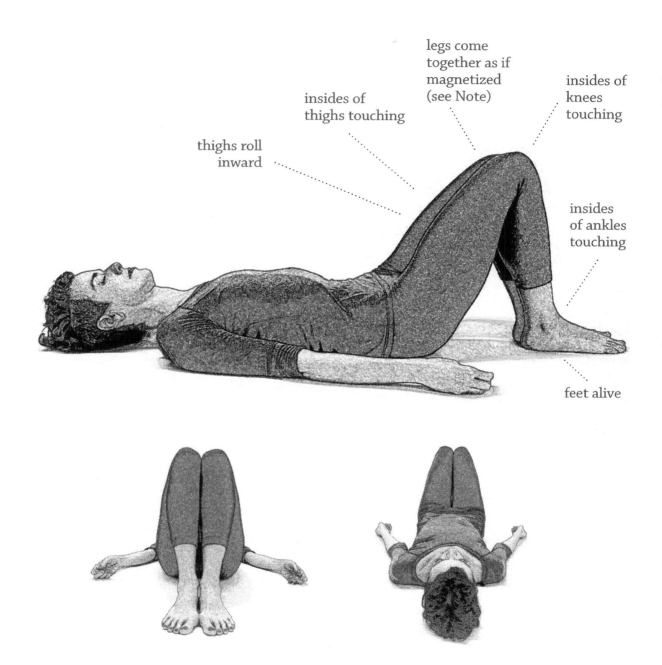

legs come together as if magnetized (see Note)

insides of thighs touching

insides of knees touching

thighs roll inward

insides of ankles touching

feet alive

The BREATH Notice your breathing. Gently encourage your exhalations to become longer and your inhalations to become shorter (reference on page 35). Find softness in both.

Spinal Flip

PRACTICE POINTS

- Cultivating the 4 Qualities of movement is more important than the movement itself.

- Let the tailbone be free.

- Increase the vigor of the movement by reducing effort, not increasing it.

- The field expands outward from the body, not from a mental image.

NOTE

- This Movement is done at the beginning and end of every practice.

- It is important to breath through the nose. Keep lips lightly sealed.

- Imagine the spine and discs opening and closing like an accordion. Feel the head and pelvis moving in unison.

TEXT ON
49

SPINAL FLIP Step by Step

- Lie on your back

- Come to Mermaid Legs

- Be aware of your whole body

- Move your lower back toward the floor as you tip your chin toward the ceiling

- Lift your lower back away from the floor as you bring your chin toward your chest

- Alternate quickly and rhythmically between these two movements, exhaling when your back moves toward the floor

- Spurt

- Stop

LIGHT | SPRINGY | RHYTHMIC | REFLEXIVE   *Developing the Qualities is 70% of the practice.*

EXHALE

MERMAID LEGS

chin rises,
neck arches

head rolls
back

pelvis rolls
toward head

FEET AND
BACK BODY
ALIVE

back moves
toward floor

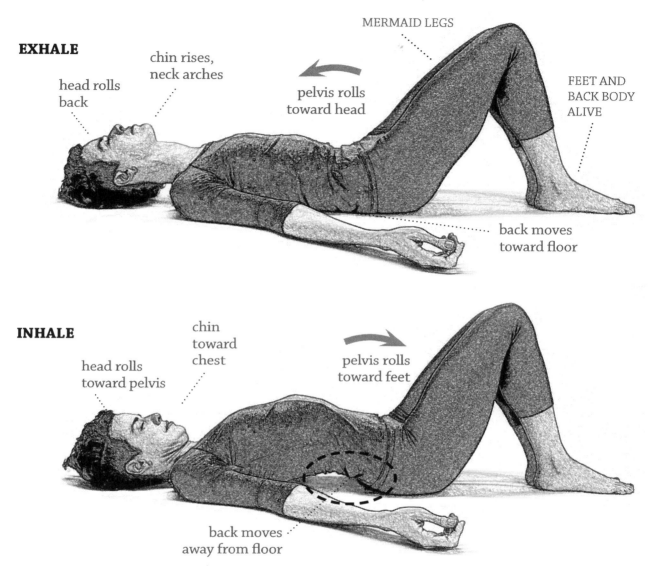

INHALE

chin
toward
chest

head rolls
toward pelvis

pelvis rolls
toward feet

back moves
away from floor

Alternate Quickly with RHYTHMIC Movements

The BREATH The breath and body are fused together in a vigorous movement.

STOP      1-3 minutes

Crossed Leg Spinal Flip

PRACTICE POINTS

- Be aware of the spine from the tip of the tailbone to the skull.
- Feel the interplay between the pelvis, ribcage and skull.
- Maintain an internal rotation of the thighs and strong, clear Mermaid Legs.

REFINEMENTS

When the right leg is crossed over the left, the line of the movement travels through the torso slightly right of the spine; when the left leg is crossed over the right, the movement line is just to the left side of the spine.

CROSSED LEG SPINAL FLIP Step by Step

- Lie on your back
- Come to Mermaid Legs crossing your right leg over your left
- Be aware of the connection of your left foot to the floor
- Keep your right foot slightly flexed
- Move your lower back toward the floor as you tip your chin toward the ceiling
- Lift your lower back away from the floor as you bring your chin toward your chest
- Alternate quickly and rhythmically between these two movements, exhaling when your back moves toward the floor
- Spurt
- Stop

- Do the movement on the other side

LIGHT | SPRINGY | RHYTHMIC | REFLEXIVE   *Developing the Qualities is 70% of the practice.*

Crossed Leg Spinal Flip

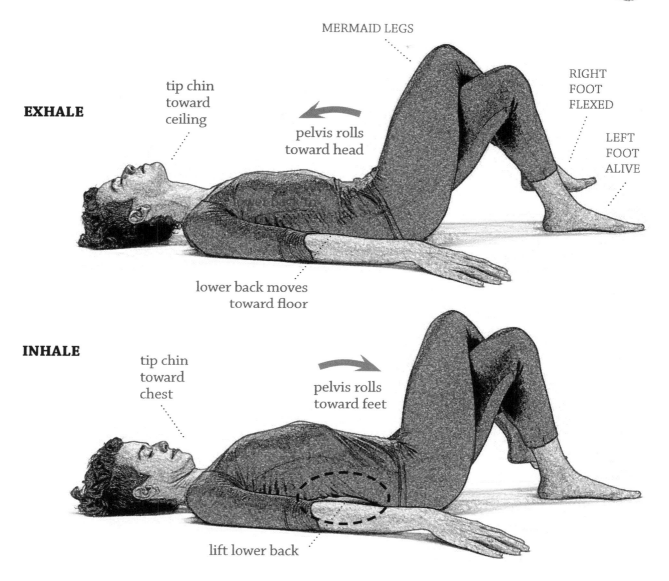

MERMAID LEGS

EXHALE

tip chin
toward
ceiling

pelvis rolls
toward head

RIGHT
FOOT
FLEXED

LEFT
FOOT
ALIVE

lower back moves
toward floor

INHALE

tip chin
toward
chest

pelvis rolls
toward feet

lift lower back

Alternate Quickly with LIGHT Movements

The BREATH   The exhale movement and the exhalation end at the same moment.
The inhalation takes care of itself.

STOP      1-3 minutes

SI Tap

PRACTICE POINTS

- Let the ribcage stay open, soft and responsive.
- The exhalation and movement end together as a staccato downbeat.
- In Stopping, expect to be nourished by prana.

NOTE

"SI" refers to the sacroiliac joint.

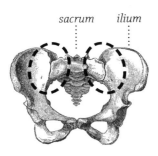

sacrum   ilium

REFINEMENTS

The pelvic bone rebounds from the floor in a light and springy way. No heaviness or dullness in the tapping.

SI TAP Step by Step

- Lie on your back
- Come to Mermaid Legs
- Lift your pelvis, rotate it slightly to the right, and tap it on the floor
- Lift, rotate to the left, and tap it on the floor
- Let the tapping motion be light and springy
- Feel the rotation in your waist
- Alternate lightly and rhythmically between these two movements
- Exhale as you tap
- Spurt
- Stop

LIGHT | SPRINGY | RHYTHMIC | REFLEXIVE   *Developing the Qualities is 70% of the practice.*

MERMAID LEGS

SENSE THE
MIDLINE

lift pelvis a couple
inches off the floor

rotate and
tap pelvis
on the right

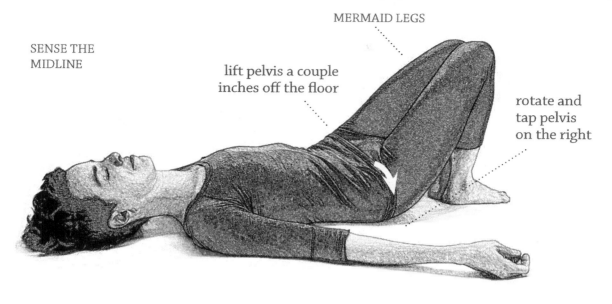

**EXHALE
as you tap**

lift, rotate and tap
pelvis on the left

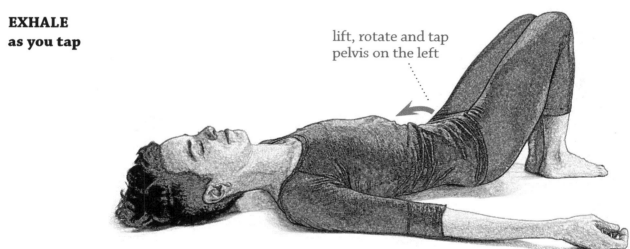

Alternate Quickly with SPRINGY Movements

The BREATH The exhale movement is like a bellows, it pushes the breath out of the body.
The inhalation takes care of itself.

STOP  1-3 minutes

Pelvic Figure 8

PRACTICE POINTS

- Maintain awareness of your whole body while moving.

- You are cultivating both strength and lightness in the legs. Look for the lightness.

- Stopping is as important as moving.

REFINEMENTS

- The Figure 8 can vary in size from a small contained movement close to the sacrum – to a large pelvic movement that actively involves the rib cage and thoracic spine.

- The legs maintain an intimate relationship to each other. The feeling of "magnetization" is present even though the legs are slightly separated.

PELVIC FIGURE 8 Step by Step

- Lie on your back

- Come to Mermaid Legs with your legs over your belly

- Remember to maintain Mermaid Legs

- Make a figure eight movement with your pelvis

- Cultivate the flow of a figure eight movement

- Find a fluid feeling of a figure 8 rather than trying to create a perfect figure 8

- Allow the movement to go through your whole spine

- Exhale on one side

- Spurt

- Stop

LIGHT | SPRINGY | RHYTHMIC | REFLEXIVE *Developing the Qualities is 70% of the practice.*

MAKE A FIGURE
8 MOVEMENT

MERMAID
LEGS

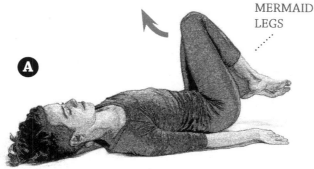

A

SENSE THE
MOVEMENT IN
LOWER BACK

EXHALE
to one side

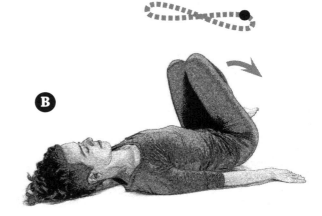

B

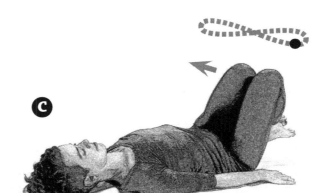

C

RHYTHMIC Movements

The BREATH The body and breath are fused, not coordinated

STOP  1-3 minutes

Belly Pump

PRACTICE POINTS

- Let the heart float, let it stay buoyant throughout moving and stopping.
- The body and breath are powerfully unified.
- The size and dynamics of the field will change depending on the movement.

NOTE

The legs maintain an intimate relationship to each other. The feeling of "magnetization" is present even though the legs are slightly separated.

REFINEMENTS

This is a communication between the belly and thigh. Sense the belly opening to receive the pressure of the thigh.

BELLY PUMP Step by Step

- Lie on your back
- Come to Mermaid Legs with your legs slightly separated
- Bring your left knee over the belly
- Clasp your knee with your hands
- Draw your thigh toward your belly on the exhale
- Release your thigh away from the belly on the inhale
- Alternate rhythmically between these two movements, exhaling when your knee moves toward the belly
- Spurt
- Stop
- Repeat Movement with right leg

LIGHT | SPRINGY | RHYTHMIC | REFLEXIVE *Developing the Qualities is 70% of the practice.*

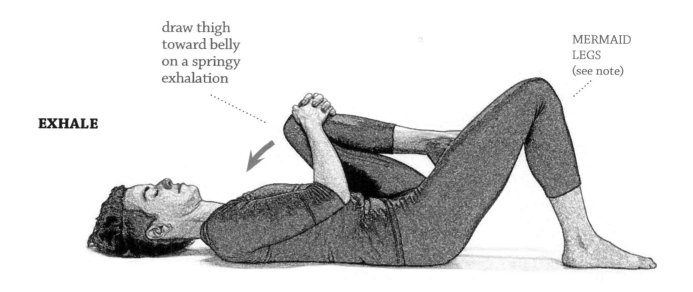

EXHALE

draw thigh toward belly on a springy exhalation

MERMAID LEGS (see note)

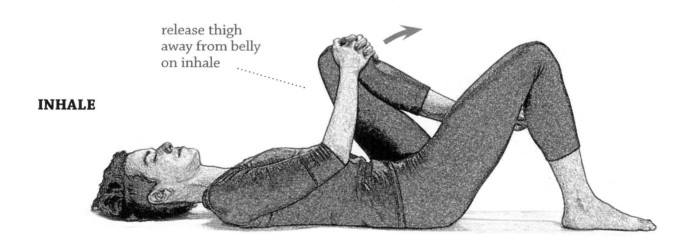

INHALE

release thigh away from belly on inhale

Alternate Quickly with SPRINGY Movements

The BREATH The breath is vigorous *and* light

STOP  1-3 minutes

Wood Chop

PRACTICE POINTS

- The exhalation ends exactly at the same moment as the exhale movement.

- Let the eyes stay soft, fluid and unfocused.

- As much as possible, maintain a no-thought mind during Stopping, and in the transition from moving into Stopping. Thinking reduces the stimulation of prana and so diminishes the benefits of Stopping.

REFINEMENTS

The shoulder girdle and rib cage remain quiet and stable in order to support a strong, vigorous action of the arms.

WOOD CHOP Step by Step

- Lie on your back

- Come to Mermaid Legs

- Extend your arms toward the ceiling and interlace your fingers

- Keep your elbows straight

- Make a staccato chopping movement of the arms toward your legs

- Let the arms spring back to their starting position

- Exhale on the chop

- Inhale on the rebound

- Spurt

- Stop

LIGHT | SPRINGY | RHYTHMIC | REFLEXIVE *Developing the Qualities is 70% of the practice.*

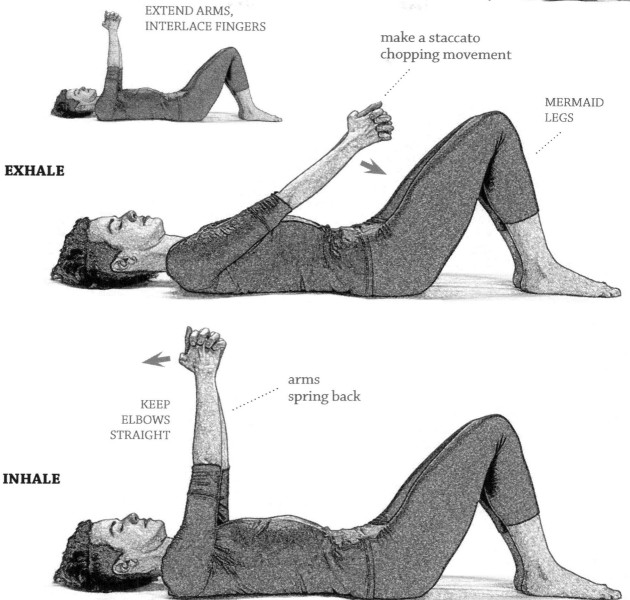

EXTEND ARMS,
INTERLACE FINGERS

make a staccato
chopping movement

MERMAID
LEGS

EXHALE

arms
spring back

KEEP
ELBOWS
STRAIGHT

INHALE

Alternate Quickly with REFLEXIVE Movements

The BREATH Breathe through the nose; the lips stay closed

STOP  1-3 minutes

Arm Slide

PRACTICE POINTS

- The breath and body have a matched intensity while moving.
- Remember the qualities and find one that helps your movement.
- In Stopping, sense prana around your body and release yourself into it. It is like floating.

ARM SLIDE Step by Step

- Lie on your back
- Come to Mermaid Legs
- Rest your arms on the floor alongside your body, palms facing down
- Alternate sliding one arm and then the other in the direction of your feet
- Exhale on one side only
- Alternate rhythmically between these two movements
- Spurt
- Stop

LIGHT | SPRINGY | RHYTHMIC | REFLEXIVE   *Developing the Qualities is 70% of the practice.*

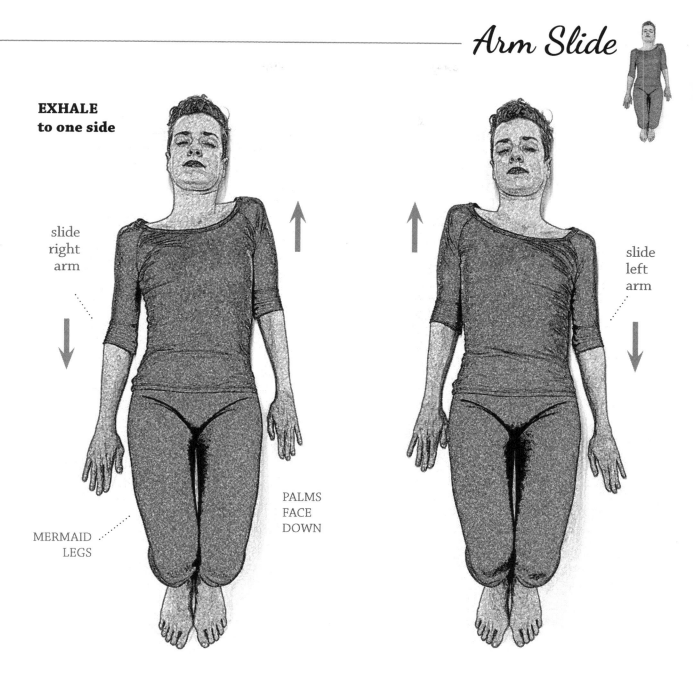

**EXHALE
to one side**

slide
right
arm

slide
left
arm

MERMAID
LEGS

PALMS
FACE
DOWN

Alternate Quickly with LIGHT Movements

The BREATH The back of the lower abdomen is engaged during breathing

STOP   1-3 minutes

Shoulder Figure 8

PRACTICE POINTS

- Every movement is a whole-body movement.

- Let the lips stay sealed and the throat relaxed open.

- In Stopping, trust and open yourself to prana. Let it flow through you in any way it wants.

REFINEMENTS

- Reduce effort.
- Do it like a child playing.
- The arms rotate along their length and the shoulder blades slide freely on the back ribs. Invite the vertebrae between the shoulder blades to participate.

SHOULDER FIGURE 8 Step by Step

- Lie on your back

- Come to Mermaid Legs

- Extend your arms to the ceiling and interlace your fingers

- Keep your elbows straight

- Make a figure eight movement by rotating your hands, arms and shoulder girdle

- Exhale on one side

- Spurt

- Stop

LIGHT | SPRINGY | RHYTHMIC | REFLEXIVE   *Developing the Qualities is 70% of the practice.*

Shoulder Figure 8

MAKE A FIGURE 8
MOVEMENT

MERMAID
LEGS

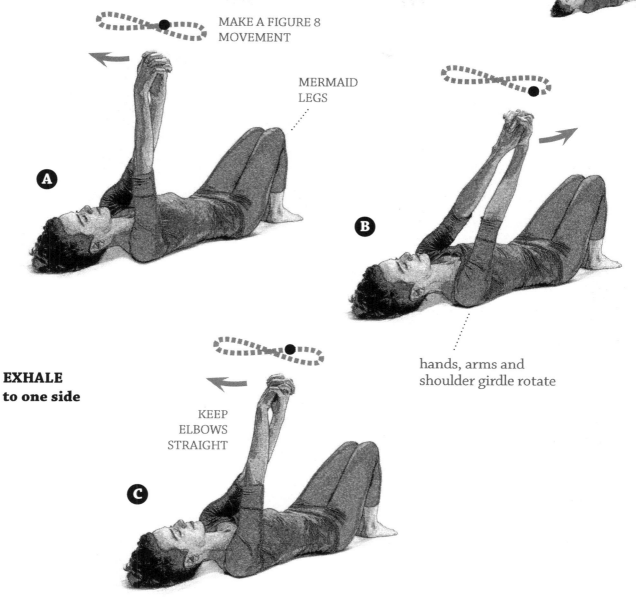

A

B

hands, arms and
shoulder girdle rotate

EXHALE
to one side

C

KEEP
ELBOWS
STRAIGHT

RHYTHMIC Movements

The BREATH The body and breath press into each other, each strengthening the other

STOP  1-3 minutes

Clamshell

PRACTICE POINTS

- You are cultivating both strength and ease of movement. Look for lightness within the strength of the movement.

- Let the skin on the skull remain soft.

- Feel the sweetness that comes in fully Stopping.

REFINEMENTS

- The rhythm of Clamshell is a strong and reflexive snapping of the legs together on the exhale, with a slight softening of the legs as they open on the inhalation.

- Actively engage the muscles of inner arms and thighs, leaving the outer ones passive. The torso remains quiet. The shoulder and hips joints stay soft.

CLAMSHELL Step by Step

- Lie on your back

- Interlace your fingers and cradle your head, keeping the backs of your hands in contact with the floor

- Open your knees and elbows away from each other

- Bring the inside edges of your feet in contact with each other

- "Clap" your legs and elbows toward each other as you exhale

- Open your legs and elbows away from each other as you inhale

- Spurt

- Stop

LIGHT | SPRINGY | RHYTHMIC | REFLEXIVE *Developing the Qualities is 70% of the practice.*

CRADLE HEAD
WITH HANDS

HANDS
ON FLOOR

INHALE

EXHALE

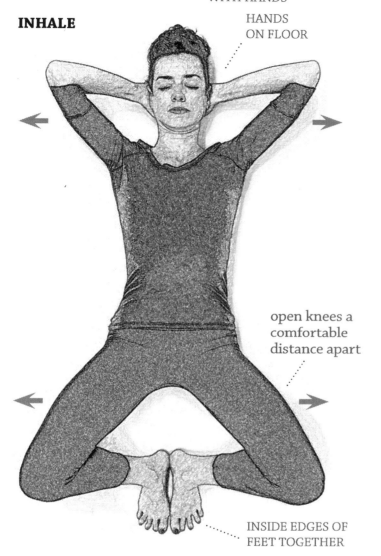

clap
elbows
toward
each
other

open knees a
comfortable
distance apart

clap legs
together

INSIDE EDGES OF
FEET TOGETHER

Alternate Quickly with REFLEXIVE Movements

The BREATH Lift the soft palate to ease the flow of breath.

STOP  1-3 minutes

Alternating Clamshell

PRACTICE POINTS

- Initiate the movement with the skeleton rather than the muscles.
- Strain in the mind or body is counterproductive. If any appears, rest until you are at ease, then continue.
- In Stopping, surrender to the support of prana.

NOTE

- Enjoy the confusion, like when you were a child!
- Take as many short breaks as needed to maintain inner quiet and a gentle curiosity.
- Read more about this Movement as a Neurological Cleanser, page 126.

ALTERNATING CLAMSHELL Step by Step

- Lie on your back
- Interlace your fingers and cradle your head, keeping the backs of your hands in contact with the floor
- Bring the inside edges of your feet in contact with each other
- Bring your elbows toward each other and leave your knees open a comfortable distance.
- Open the elbows out to the side while simultaneously clapping the knees toward each other
- Continue opening and clapping the arms and legs in opposition
- If you become confused take a brief rest and then return to the movement
- Spurt
- Stop

LIGHT | SPRINGY | RHYTHMIC | REFLEXIVE   *Developing the Qualities is 70% of the practice.*

Alternating Clamshell

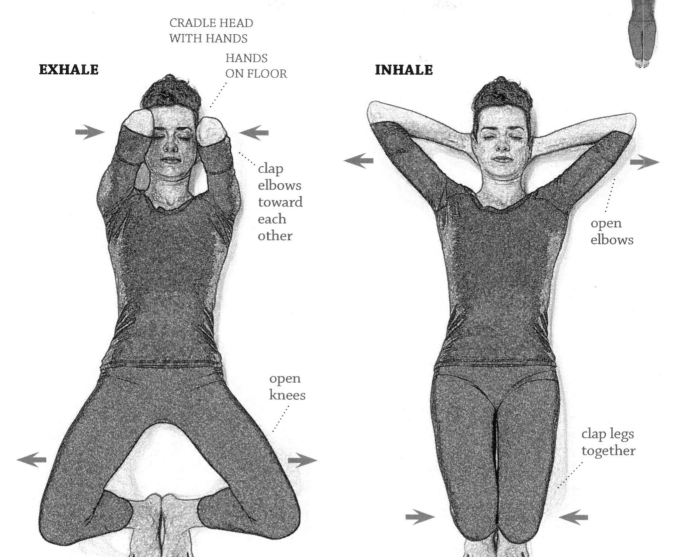

EXHALE

CRADLE HEAD WITH HANDS

HANDS ON FLOOR

clap elbows toward each other

open knees

INSIDE EDGES OF FEET TOGETHER

INHALE

open elbows

clap legs together

Alternate Quickly with LIGHT Movements

The BREATH   Breathing comes from the spine

STOP   1-3 minutes

Snake

PRACTICE POINTS

- Increase the vigor of the movement by reducing effort, not increasing it.

- Keep your lips sealed and maintain a soft space between your upper and lower back teeth.

- You are stimulating prana with the breath and movement. Stimulated prana expresses in different ways. There is no 'right' way.

REFINEMENTS

- Let your back stay connected to the floor and receive the sensation of that contact while moving.

- Imagine a snake and how intimate it is with the ground.

SNAKE Step by Step

- Lie on your back
- Come to Mermaid Legs with your legs over your belly
- Interlace your fingers and cradle your head in your hands
- Use your hands to lift your head very slightly off the floor
- Rest your head into the support of the hands
- Flex your body from side to side, bringing your elbow and hip toward each other each time
- Alternate lightly and rhythmically between these side-to-side movements
- Choose one side for your exhalation
- Spurt
- Stop

LIGHT | SPRINGY | RHYTHMIC | REFLEXIVE   *Developing the Qualities is 70% of the practice.*

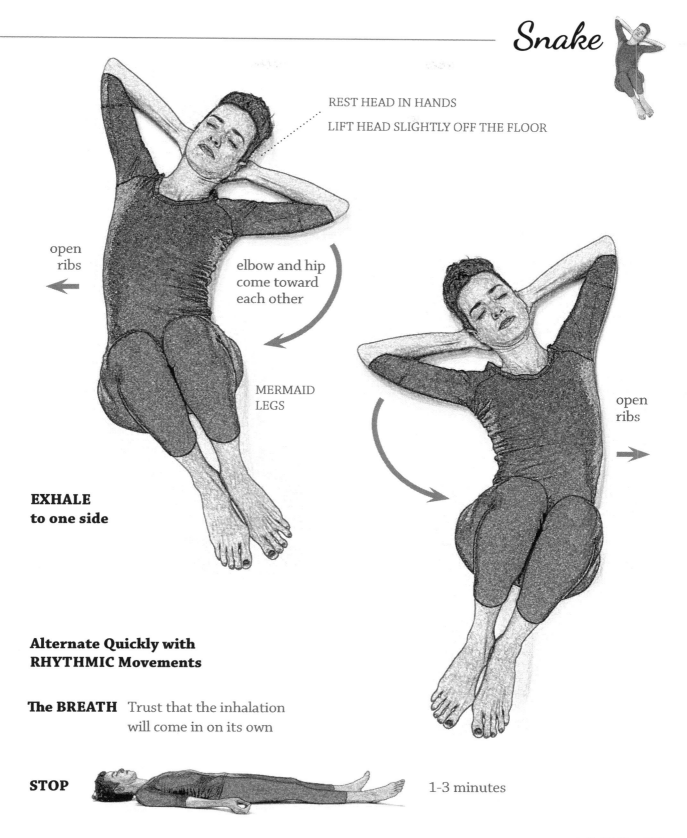

REST HEAD IN HANDS

LIFT HEAD SLIGHTLY OFF THE FLOOR

open
ribs

←

elbow and hip
come toward
each other

MERMAID
LEGS

EXHALE
to one side

open
ribs

→

Alternate Quickly with
RHYTHMIC Movements

The BREATH Trust that the inhalation
will come in on its own

STOP

1-3 minutes

Spring

PRACTICE POINTS

- Vitality comes not from effort, but from cultivating dynamic springiness and reflexivity.

- Let your brain relax into the back of your skull.

- Sense awakened prana cleansing and nourishing you during Stopping.

REFINEMENTS

- This Movement is initiated by spring-like action in the torso. The arms and legs contribute strongly, but are secondary.

- The legs maintain an intimate relationship to each other. The feeling of "magnetization" is present even though the legs are slightly separated.

SPRING Step by Step

- Lie on your back

- Bring your legs over your belly – separated enough to allow your arms to move between them, but they maintain a Mermaid Legs dynamic

- Extend your arms to the ceiling and interlace your fingers

- Keep your elbows straight

- Make a staccato chopping movement toward your legs while you bring your legs toward your arms

- The arms move between the legs

- Let the arms and legs spring back to their starting position

- Exhale on the chop

- Inhale on the rebound

- Spurt

- Stop

LIGHT | SPRINGY | RHYTHMIC | REFLEXIVE *Developing the Qualities is 70% of the practice.*

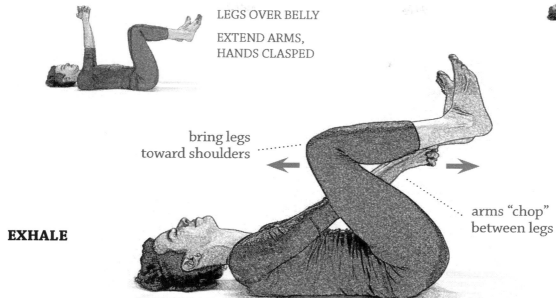

LEGS OVER BELLY

EXTEND ARMS, HANDS CLASPED

bring legs toward shoulders

arms "chop" between legs

EXHALE

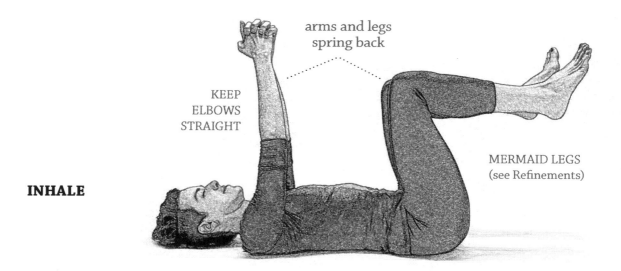

arms and legs spring back

KEEP ELBOWS STRAIGHT

MERMAID LEGS (see Refinements)

INHALE

Alternate Quickly with REFLEXIVE Movements

The BREATH Focusing on the point between your eyes stabilizes the breath

STOP   1-3 minutes

Torso Walk

PRACTICE POINTS

- The four qualities refine your body and the Movement.

- Let your body be carried by the rhythm of the Movement.

- Deeply absorb prana in Stopping.

NOTE

- Pay attention to the interplay between the shoulders and the pelvis, letting them be evenly engaged. This Movement enlivens the rotation of the torso.

- Find the feeling of walking in the center of the torso and find a synchronous movement of the shoulders and hips.

TORSO WALK Step by Step

- Lie on your back

- Bring both legs over the belly

- The legs are slightly apart but maintained in a Mermaid Leg dynamic

- Cup your knees with your hands

- Alternate bringing one leg and then the other toward the torso in a vigorous, whole-body movement

- Maintain awareness of the connection of your back to the floor

- Choose one side for the exhalation; exhale as the thigh comes toward the torso

- Spurt

- Stop

LIGHT | SPRINGY | RHYTHMIC | REFLEXIVE   *Developing the Qualities is 70% of the practice.*

LEGS OVER BELLY,
CUP KNEES

MERMAID
LEGS

bring
right thigh
toward
torso

EXHALE
to one side

bring left thigh
toward torso

vigorous,
whole-body
movement

Alternate Quickly with SPRINGY Movements

The BREATH The aliveness of the feet support freedom in the breath

 STOP  1-3 minutes

Walking

PRACTICE POINTS

- The feet are alive and supportive as in dancing. They are not planted.
- Imagine smelling a rose and sense how the inside of the nose enlivens. Maintain that enlivening through the whole movement.
- Let your cells receive prana in Stopping.

NOTE

- Mermaid Legs is a dynamic relationship between the legs. It is easiest to learn when the legs are actually touching, but the dynamic can be found in any position.
- After you connect to the feeling of walking and find a harmonious walking-like movement of the arms and legs; let yourself rest deeply in that rhythm – let it carry you in the Movement.

WALKING Step by Step

- Lie on your back
- Bend your legs, with feet parallel and knees a couple of inches apart; maintain a Mermaid Legs dynamic
- Elongate your arms above your head on the floor
- Alternate reaching one knee and then the other in the direction it is pointed ~ imagine a button in front of each knee and you are reaching to press it
- Alternate reaching your arms
- Alternate rhythmically between these two movements; look for the familiar feeling and rhythm of a walking movement through your body
- Choose one side for the exhalation; exhale as you elongate
- Spurt
- Stop

LIGHT | SPRINGY | RHYTHMIC | REFLEXIVE   *Developing the Qualities is 70% of the practice.*

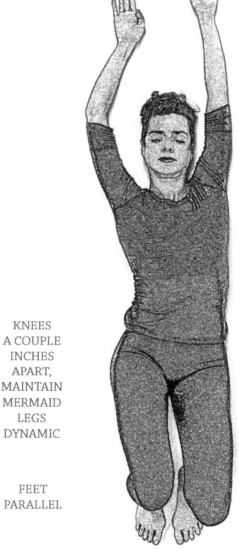

EXHALE to one side

Elongate your arm and knee away from each other

Elongate your arm and knee away from each other.

KNEES A COUPLE INCHES APART, MAINTAIN MERMAID LEGS DYNAMIC

FEET PARALLEL

Alternate Quickly with LIGHT Movements

The BREATH The 4 Qualities also apply to the breath

STOP   1-3 minutes

Neurological Cleansers

Until you are willing to be confused about what you already know,
what you know will never grow bigger, better, or more useful.
MILTON H. ERICKSON

Neurological Cleansers are Movements specifically designed as a fast-track to relieving tension.

They are based on neuromotor learning principles.

Neurological Cleansers

All 'graduations' in human (and spiritual) development
mean the abandonment of a familiar position.
ERICK H. ERIKSON

In the last chapter you were introduced to Spinal Flip, the bread-and-butter Movement of Fluid Strength. This chapter introduces you to the spices of the practice. The Neurological Cleansers are done periodically for teasing open new spaciousness and untangling habits that do not serve us.

Neurological Cleansers are based on neuromotor learning principles. These principles are woven into every aspect of Fluid Strength. Neuromotor learning principles are simply ways of using modern understanding of the brain to help us do things in an easier and more effective way.

Body- and self-awareness is the starting point for neuromotor learning. This awareness is developed by listening to the sensory information in the body. In this listening we get in touch with ourselves, which is our foundation for achieving our goals and fulfilling our lives.

NEUROLOGICAL CLEANSERS

Neurological Cleansers are Fluid Strength Movements that ask us to move in new and unusual ways. Because these movements are unfamiliar, they open new pathways in the brain and refresh the nervous system. It is close to magic how quickly they can reduce mental and physical tension.

Neurological Cleansers are a variation of Fluid Strength Movements. For the most part they are used the same way as any other Movement, although they are used sparingly. They differ in that, rather than being used to strengthen and enliven the body, their role is to help us discover more and easier ways move. Most Fluid Strength Movements are natural, neurological Cleansers are not. The Alternating Clamshell and Eye & Head Differentiation described at the end of this chapter are examples of this type of movement.

These Movements are coordination challenges. By approaching them playfully and with relaxed curiosity, they become fun and interesting. We are pleasurably surprised when we discover that these seemingly impossible movements can actually begin to feel natural.

Our cultural belief is that we can think our way through everything. Neurological Cleaners are a humbling reality check on that notion. We must feel, sense and play our way through these Movements in order to reap their benefits.

WHEN AND WHY TO DO THEM

We all have habits that can keep us distant from a comfortable, pain-free body. Neurological Cleansers can quickly disengage these habits and give us access to freer and more enjoyable movement.

Some Neurological Cleansers, like the Eye & Head Differentiation described below, can be used to great benefit almost anywhere. Done at the end of a practice they make our rest more restorative. They are great for relieving the stresses and strains that come from spending hours at a desk or other repetitive activity. With my tendency toward headaches these Movements are a godsend to me in finding relief.

Following are instructions for two Neurological Cleansers: Alternating Clamshell and Eye & Head Differentiation. Remember that the goal is not just to be able to do them, but rather to increase your self-awareness and learn to use less effort. It is about being a friend to yourself during a challenge, and remembering that if approached gently the Movements will eventually become easy and natural. The most important thing in doing Fluid Strength Movements is the quality with which they are done. (See Qualities of Movement chapter, page 77.) With the Eye Movements, gentleness is essential.

Alternating Clamshell

ALTERNATING CLAMSHELL (also on page 114)

- Lie on your back
- Interlace your fingers and cradle your head, keeping the backs of your hands in contact with the floor
- Bring the inside edges of your feet in contact with each other
- Bring your elbows toward each other and leave your knees open a comfortable distance.
- Open the elbows out to the side while simultaneously clapping the knees toward each other
- Continue opening and clapping the arms and legs in opposition
- If you become confused take a brief rest and then return to the movement
- Spurt
- Stop

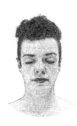

EYE & HEAD DIFFERENTIATION

Lie comfortably on your back.

Rest for a moment with your eyes closed.

Let your eyes open with a soft focus.

⫸ MOVE HEAD & EYES TOGETHER ⫷

- Gently roll your head a tiny amount to the right, letting your eyes and head move together

- Roll head and eyes back to center

- Gently roll your head to the left, letting your eyes move with the head

- Roll your head and eyes back to center

- Repeat this movement a number of times focusing on letting it be easy and pleasant

- Close the eyes and rest

⫸ MOVE HEAD & EYES IN OPPOSITION ⫷

- Begin rolling your head slightly to the right as you roll your eyes to the left

- Continue rolling your head left and right while the eyes are rolling in the opposite direction

- Notice when the eyes and head start to move together then pause for a moment and return to the opposing eye and head movements

- If you feel any effort or agitation rest for a bit, then return to the movement

- Move gently, softly, even lazily, and be aware of the sensation of the eyes and head moving

- Rest

- Repeat

- Move the head and eyes together

- Rest

Ten thousand flowers in spring,
the moon in autumn, a cool
breeze in summer, snow in
winter,
If your mind isn't clouded by
unnecessary things, this is the
best season of your life.
WU-MEN

Between stimulus and response
there is a space. In that space
is our power to choose our
response. In our response lies
our growth and our freedom.
VIKTOR E. FRANKL

Practice Options

Sometimes it is a time constraint that determines our practice. This section gives you **four practice options** based on time: a 5-minute, 15-minute, 30-minute and a 60-minute practice. Once you become familiar with the Movements, you can create your own practice using your favorite Movements. Although don't avoid your least favorite!

The 15-minute practice is a good place to start. It will take a little longer until you are familiar with the Movements. The 5-minute practice is quick and effective for energizing and centering yourself when you are short on time. Remember to start with Transitional Awareness and end with Stopping.

5-Minute Practice

Practice time varies with each Movement.

We've put small images in the upper right corner of the the book to help you find a Movement.

TRANSITIONAL AWARENESS ~ PAGE 93

SPINAL FLIP ~ PAGE 96

(MERMAID LEGS IS ON PAGE 94)

STOP ~ PAGE 63

15-Minute Practice

TRANSITIONAL AWARENESS ~ PAGE 93

SPINAL FLIP ~
PAGE 96

(MERMAID LEGS PAGE 94)

CLAMSHELL ~ PAGE 112

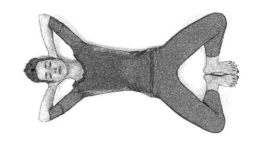

WOOD CHOP ~
PAGE 106

SPRING ~ PAGE 118

STOP ~ PAGE 63

30-Minute Practice

TRANSITIONAL AWARENESS ~ PAGE 93

SPINAL FLIP ~
PAGE 96

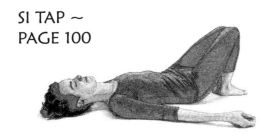

(MERMAID LEGS PAGE 94)

SI TAP ~
PAGE 100

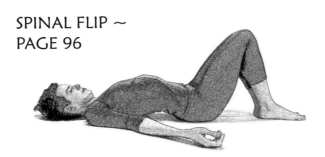

WOOD CHOP ~
PAGE 106

CLAMSHELL ~ PAGE 112

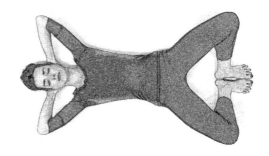

ALTERNATING CLAMSHELL ~
PAGE 114

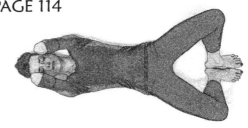

SNAKE ~ PAGE 116

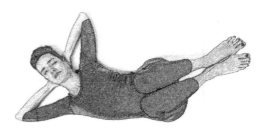

SPRING ~
PAGE 118

TORSO WALK ~
PAGE 120

STOP ~ PAGE 63

For videos of the
Fluid Strength
Movements –
fluid-strength-
yoga-practice.com

60-Minute Practice

TRANSITIONAL AWARENESS ~ PAGE 93

SPINAL FLIP ~
PAGE 96

PELVIC FIGURE 8 ~
PAGE 102

CROSSED LEG SPINAL FLIP ~
PAGE 98

BELLY PUMP ~ PAGE 104

SI TAP ~
PAGE 100

ARM SLIDE ~ PAGE 108

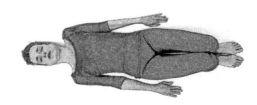

SHOULDER FIGURE 8 ~ PAGE 110

CLAMSHELL ~ PAGE 112

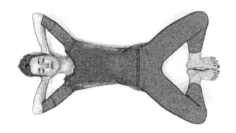

ALTERNATING CLAMSHELL ~ PAGE 114

SPRING ~ PAGE 118

TORSO WALK ~ PAGE 120

EYE & HEAD DIFFERENTIATION ~ PAGE 129

STOP ~ PAGE 63

Movement Index

*This section gives you an overview of the **Movements** with descriptions of some of their unique benefits. All Movements discussed in this book appear here in alphabetical order except for Mermaid Legs and Transitional Awareness which appear at the beginning, and Stopping which appears at the end.*

You can use this index to get a general sense of the practice. It is also a handy reference for choosing Movements to explore, or for designing yourself a practice.

If we do not pay attention to ourselves in our practice, then we cannot call it yoga.
T. K. V. DESIKACHAR

Movement Index

TRANSITIONAL AWARENESS

Each Fluid Strength practice starts with Transitional Awareness as a way of bringing oneself to the present moment. This process releases physical tension, calms the mind, and puts you into a relationship with yourself that helps to maximize the benefits of your practice. It can be done in a few minutes to brush off the dust of the day, or it can be done on its own for 20 minutes as a restorative practice.

MERMAID LEGS

Mermaid Legs is the foundation of every Fluid Strength Movement. It merges the strength of the legs, vitalizes the spine and balances the two sides of the body. It is the anchor for creating powerful movements of the torso. Resting in Mermaid Legs with awareness of the midline is a physical meditation.

ARM SLIDE

We can sometimes feel we are carrying the weight of the world on our shoulders, taking the form of chronic tension and pain. This Movement brings a freedom and lightness to the shoulder girdle and upper back. It will lift and lighten your mood.

BELLY PUMP

Belly Pump promotes healthy digestive function which in turn supports whole body health. This belly massage stimulates the digestive organs and relieves abdominal tension.

CLAMSHELL

Clamshell is a powerful movement that will energize you while cultivating confidence and strength. It releases tension and stiffness from shoulders and hips, restoring freedom to the arms and legs.

CLAMSHELL, ALTERNATING

This non-habitual movement taps into your potential for new options and choices. The feeling of confusion arising from Alternating Clamshell means that you are doing something new and beneficial. It can help you when you are feeling stuck.

EYES & HEAD DIFFERENTIATION

Once you are comfortable with the eye movements they can be used in almost any situation to release tension. Done at the end of a practice they deepen our rest. They are great for preventing or relieving head and neck stress from long hours of sitting. They can be a godsend for relieving headaches. With these movements small and gentle is the key.

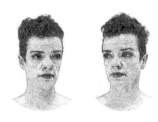

FIGURE EIGHT – PELVIC

The figure eight brings playfulness to the body and mind. It can help you to cultivate a joyful attitude and awaken your creativity.

The pelvis and thighs are the center of our physical power. The **Pelvic Figure Eight** energizes and enlivens these large muscles. It connects us to our physical strength, mobilizes the hips joints, and massages the lower back.

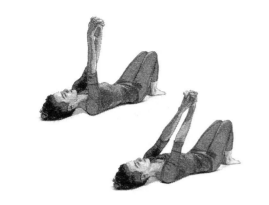

FIGURE EIGHT – SHOULDER

The **Shoulder Figure Eight** mobilizes the shoulder girdle, restores full range of movement to the arms, and connects the arms to the strength of the back. The arms are considered an extension of the heart, and this Movement gives the heart a healthy massage.

RIB-CAGE-TAP BREATHING

The diaphragm is our main breathing muscle. It can easily become stuck or restricted due to respiratory illness or mental and emotional stress. These Movements free up the diaphragm, facilitating full, whole body breathing. It will enliven your body and restore a sense of well-being.

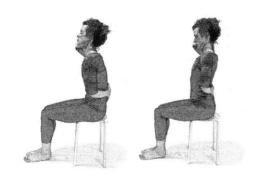

SEATED SPINAL AWARENESS

Seated Spinal Awareness is the first step on the path to spinal health and vitality. It will remind you that the structure running through your center of support is fluid, strong, and full of potential. Use it to release tension while working/sitting for long stretches of time at a desk, and anytime you need to center yourself.

SI TAP (SACRO ILIAC)

SI Tap literally wakes up the base of your spine and pelvis, which can easily feel dull and locked. It revitalizes the whole spine, frees the hip joints, and strengthens the legs.

SNAKE

Snake is a dynamic whole body movement. It provides a therapeutic side flexion to the spine and a healthy compression/release for all the internal organs. Snake will energize you and help you to cultivate whole body strength and coordination. Practice Snake when you want to develop concentration, and when you literally want to pull yourself together.

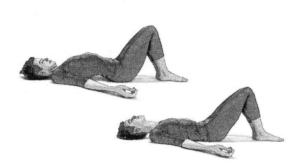

SPINAL FLIP

Spinal Flip is the core Movement in Fluid Strength that literally brings you home to yourself. The perfect tonic for body and mind, this beautiful spinal movement will:

- Mobilize and warm the spine
- Release physical and mental tension
- Relieve pain
- Dissolve anxiety

SPINAL FLIP, CROSSED LEG

Spinal Flip can be initiated in multiple ways. This keeps the Movement bright and fresh, your mind engaged, and guards against habitual ways of moving which can make the mind dull.

SPRING

The whole body functions as a spring in this vigorous movement. We think of it as the fountain of youth! As the spine is squeezed and released, the vertebral discs are hydrated and rejuvenated, vitalizing and mobilizing the spine.

TORSO WALK

Torso Walk massages the belly and spine. It supports healthy digestion. The interplay of the limbs enlivens the torso and integrates the arms and shoulders with the legs and hips. It helps to clear the slate of tension, stress, and worry.

WALKING

Walking recreates the enjoyment and ease of a natural walking movement. By doing it on the floor, the spine is relieved of its usual supportive function and is free to discover its full capacity for whole body movement.

WOODCHOP

Woodchop is a no-nonsense Movement that cultivates clarity and a sense of purpose. It connects you to the strength of your midline, and to your innate power and capability.

STOPPING

Stopping gives our body and mind a chance to regain equilibrium, and the space to remember that our life is in the present moment. It is used after every Fluid Strength Movement. It awakens a quality of rest reminiscent of floating in water. Stopping is a place in which we can enjoy a still body, a mind free from thought, spacious awareness, and an attitude of surrender.

Resources

YOGA

Awakening the Spine: The Stress-Free New Yoga that Works with the Body to Restore Health, Vitality and Energy
Vanda Scaravelli

The Mirror of Yoga: Awakening the Intelligence of Body and Mind
Richard Freeman

The Inner Tradition of Yoga: A Guide to Yoga Philosophy for the Contemporary Practitioner
Michael Stone, Richard Freeman (Foreword)

Japanese Yoga: The Way of Dynamic Meditation
H. E. Davey

Tibetan Yoga of Movement: The Art and Practice of Yantra Yoga
Chogyal Namkhai Norbu, Fabio Andrico

The Complete Book of Oriental Yoga: Hatha and Taoist Yoga for the Seasons
Michael Hetherington

Tibetan Yoga of Movement: Perfect Rhythm of Life - Level One DVD
Fabio Andrico (Actor), Laura Evangelisti (Actor), Tatyana Khodakivska (Director)

NEUROMOTOR LEARNING

Awareness Through Movement: Easy-to-Do Health Exercises to Improve Your Posture, Vision, Imagination, and Personal Awareness
Moshe Feldenkrais

Awareness Heals: The Feldenkrais Method for Dynamic Health
Stephen Shafarman

Relaxercise: The Easy New Way to Health and Fitness
David Zemach-Bersin, Kaethe Zemach-Bersin, Mark Reese

feldenkrais.com
feldenkraisresources.com
movementintelligence.org

AYURVEDA

The Complete Book of Ayurvedic Home Remedies: Based on the Timeless Wisdom of India's 5,000-Year-Old Medical System
Vasant Lad

Ayurveda, Nature's Medicine
David Dr. Frawley & Subhash Dr. Ranade
www.ayurveda.com

BREATH

Free Your Breath, Free Your Life: How Conscious Breathing Can Relieve Stress, Increase Vitality, and Help You Live More Fully
Dennis Lewis

Breathe To Heal: Break Free From Asthma – Learn Buteyko
Sasha Yakovleva, K.P. Buteyko MD-PhD, A.E. Novozhilov MD

buteykoclinic.com

EMBODIED AWARENESS

Wisdom of the Body Moving: An Introduction to Body-Mind Centering
Linda Hartley

bodymindcentering.com
continuummovement.com

Contributors to this Book

Faye Berton, MA

Faye has been teaching yoga and working with The Feldenkrais Method® since 1988. She has the highest certification from Yoga Alliance and is a FGNA certified Feldenkrais practitioner. She holds certifications through the Ayurvedic Institute as an Ayurvedic Consultant and through the Foundation for Movement Intelligence as a Bones for Life® practitioner.

Karin, Mary Ann, Faye and Jean

After establishing the Laurel Yoga Studio in St. Paul, Minnesota, she moved to Mexico and opened Casa Lalita Retreat Center. For 13 years she taught between Mexico, USA and Canada. After 23 years of teaching traditional asana she developed the Fluid Strength Yoga Practice. She now lives in St. Paul, where she teaches The Fluid Strength Yoga Practice, does private sessions in The Feldenkrais Method, and develops health and wellness workshops.

Her studies in yoga philosophy were through The Himalayan Tradition as taught by Swami Nijananda Bharati and Swami Veda Bharati. Her training in asana is extensive and varied. Some of the world masters of somatic disciplines with whom she has trained include Marjorie Barstow, Emile Conrad, Charlotte Selver, Else Middendorf and Ruthy Alon.

Jean Fraser, CYT

Over 30 years of experience in therapeutic movement, dance, and yoga inform Jean's teaching. Her current interest is in refining movement practices into accessible tools for addressing anxiety and stress.

She began her yoga education with Faye Berton in 1994. Her influences include somatic work with Nancy Topf and yoga teacher training with Donna Farhi. Jean's personal journey led her back to Faye (as described in this book) where she continues her study of Fluid Strength.

Jean has extended her work into community health and wellness organizations by training health care professionals to incorporate movement-based skills into their work with clients.

Jean designed and teaches the yoga component of Dr. Henry Emmons' Pathways to Resilience courses. She authored the yoga portion of Dr Emmons' book Staying Sharp. In 2016 Jean released her Moving Meditations CD, featuring the movement sequences she uses in her trainings. She speaks regularly at conferences for social services organizations and government agencies.

Jean is a member of the Kripalu Yoga Teachers Association, and her programs are endorsed for continuing education by the Minnesota Board of Social Work. She now joins Faye in teaching Fluid Strength at the Laurel Yoga Studio in St Paul, and is committed to sharing the Fluid Strength Yoga Practice more widely.

Karin Preus' love of design-as-communication began in 1980 with the making of posters for music clubs in Madison, Wisconsin. Following undergraduate work in Art History at UW-Madison, Karin purchased her first graphic design business, Abraxas Studio where she learned the ropes. She returned home to Minneapolis, Minnesota in 1987 where she did agency work for 10 years, working with clients such as Rollerblade, HB Fuller and Shock Doctor. In 1998 Karin founded Acorn Design.

The breadth of her creativity is expressed in the range of work for her clients, from Rollerblade corporate campaigns to Laurel Yoga Studio workshop brochures, American Diabetes Association 40-page catalogs to book design and collateral for Mitchell Hamline School of Law.

Karin creates a polished, consistent look across the spectrum of both print elements and web design. Her attention to detail, and commitment to the success of her clients make her a joy to work with. Her designs literally bring concepts and ideas to life. She is expanding her horizons once again with the publication of this book.

She lives in St. Paul with her photographer husband, Larry Marcus. She has been studying with Faye since 1994.

Mary Ann Bradley has been a professional dancer for the last twenty years. After obtaining her BA in Dance from Point Park University of Pittsburgh, PA in 1997, she moved to Minneapolis and began performing and touring with a variety of dance companies specializing in Modern, Jazz, Ballet, Ballroom, and Musical Theater. Her studies of Body Mind Centering™ and Fluid Strength™ have been integral to her career's longevity.

Contact Us

Visit our site ~ **fluid-strength-yoga-practice.com**

Information about classes, workshops and retreats at the Laurel Yoga Studio ~
laurelyogastudio.com

More about Fluid Strength and Faye Berton's work as a Feldenkrais practitioner ~
faye-berton.com

Jean Fraser's website ~ **somaventures.com**
Her **Moving Meditations** CD is available there.

Karin Preus' website ~ **acorngraphicdesign.com**

Credits

Jean Fraser ~ Editor-in-Chief

Karin Preus ~ Art Director, Graphic Designer, Movements Photographer

Mary Ann Bradley ~ Model

Larry Marcus, Photographer ~ Cover Photograph of Mary Ann
larry-marcus.com

PicturetoPeople.org ~ Movement Photo Conversions

Kathryn Charlet ~ Editor
charletk@gmail.com

Joanne Cavallaro ~ Editor

Image Credits

We are grateful to the photographers who generously share their work, and to the websites like Pexels through which they are made available.

Made in the USA
San Bernardino, CA
08 March 2018